Editorial Project Manager
Ina Massler Levin, M.A.

Editor in Chief
Sharon Coan, M.S. Ed.

Illustrator
Ken Tunell

Cover Artist
Larry Bauer

Art Coordinator
Cheri Macoubrie Wilson

Creative Director
Elayne Roberts

Imaging
Ralph Olmedo, Jr.

Product Manager
Phil Garcia

Researcher
Christine Johnson

Publishers
Rachelle Cracchiolo, M.S. Ed.
Mary Dupuy Smith, M.S. Ed.

20th CENTURY
1900-1909

Author

Dona Herweck Rice

Teacher Created Materials, Inc.
6421 Industry Way
Westminster, CA 92683
www.teachercreated.com

ISBN-1-57690-022-3

©*2000 Teacher Created Materials, Inc.*

Made in U.S.A.

Table of Contents

Table of Contents *(cont.)*

Introduction

The 20th Century is a series which examines the political, economic, social, cultural, scientific, and technological advances of the twentieth century and introduces students to individuals who made history in each decade.

1900–1909 chronicles the turn of the new century, a time promising to be a "Golden Age" filled with hope and potential. The twentieth century was seen as a new beginning, and people around the world looked to it to fulfill their dreams of peace and prosperity and a better quality of life. The times were changing rapidly, giving people the idea that nothing was impossible. Modern inventions, changing lifestyles, and different ways of thinking took hold. Expectations were high for an age replete with golden opportunity.

There was just cause for this fervor—not only because of the excitement bred at the completion of one century and the start of the next but also because of the amazing technological advances being made in almost rapid-fire succession. Although the twentieth century closes with manned flights to outer space seeming almost routine, it began with two brothers named Wright at a place called Kittyhawk. It may end with the Thrust supersonic car breaking the sound barrier, but it opened with Ford's Model T chugging along without the aid of true horsepower. It may close with blockbuster films bursting with multi-million dollar special effects, but it opened with small nickelodeons and the excitement of moving pictures. Things that are commonplace today—space travel, automotive transportation, cinema, and more—were awe-inspiring as 1900 dawned, and people waited expectantly for what "new-fangled" invention might be created next. There was no telling where the great new century would lead.

As you study the first years of the twentieth century, you will find a variety of aids in this unit to help make your studies complete, including the following:

- ❑ **a time line**—a chronology of significant events of the decade
- ❑ **planning guides**—summaries and suggested activities for introducing the key issues and events of the decade
- ❑ **personality profiles**—brief biographies of important individuals of the decade
- ❑ **world views**—chronology and details of world events of the decade
- ❑ **language experience ideas**—suggestions for writing and vocabulary building
- ❑ **group activities**—assignments to foster cooperative learning
- ❑ **topics for further research**—suggestions for extending the unit
- ❑ **literature connections**—summaries of related books and suggested activities for expanding on them
- ❑ **curriculum connections**—activities in math, art, language arts, social studies, and music
- ❑ **computer applications**—suggestions for selecting and using software to supplement this unit
- ❑ **bibliography**—suggestions for additional resources about the decade

> To keep this valuable resource intact so that it can be used year after year, you may wish to punch holes in the pages and store them in a three-ring binder.

Time Line

	1900	1901
Politics and Economics	William McKinley is president. The Boer War is in its third year. Colonel Baden-Powell fools the Boers by having young boys carry wooden weapons along the perimeter of Mafeking. Thinking the town is well defended by British troops, the Boers keep away. The Boxer Rebellion ignites in China. The rebels believe that boxing and other exercise protects them from ammunition. Hawaii is adopted as a territory of the United States. Eugene Debs announces his presidential candidacy under the newly established Social Democratic ticket. He is a supporter of laborers and a proponent of suffrage and equality.	President William McKinley is shot and killed. Vice President Theodore Roosevelt takes office, becoming the youngest president in history. Roosevelt fights against business monopolies and trusts. The six colonies of Australia unite to form a single nation. The United States begins to govern the Philippines. Future president William Taft is named governor. The Chinese government is forced to pay for the losses incurred during the Boxer Rebellion.
Social and Cultural	France hosts the Summer Olympics in Paris. The first Davis Cup in tennis is won by Dwight Davis and Holcombe Ward. The Fifth Paris Exhibit amazes the world with its demonstration of technological advances such as electric lighting. Nations from around the world submit beautiful exhibits.	England's Queen Victoria dies, closing the long Victorian Age, which began in 1837. Andrew Carnegie announces his retirement and his plan to give away his fortune in acts of philanthropy. Booker T. Washington is invited to the White House. Author Leo Tolstoy, having written against the government and religion, is blamed for student riots in Russia. The Cossacks halt the riots. The U.S. wins the America's Cup.
Science and Technology	Construction begins on the New York subway. The first Zeppelin airship takes flight. Motorcars powered by steam, electricity, and gasoline become more prevalent. By the end of the year, there are 8,000 cars on U.S. roads. Sigmund Freud's *The Interpretation of Dreams* is published.	A. E. Taylor is the first to go over Niagara Falls in a barrel. Guglielmo Marconi sends a wireless telegraphic signal across the Atlantic. Oil is discovered in Texas. A. C. Bostwick is the first to drive an automobile faster than a mile a minute.

Time Line (cont.)

1902	1903	1904
The Boer War finally draws to a close as the Boers surrender. Britain and Japan sign an agreement ensuring that Britain will not side with Russia in a dispute. A miners' strike in Pennsylvania leads to a shortage of coal throughout the nation.	King Alexander and Queen Draga of Serbia are assassinated by army officers. Turkish papers report the couple died of indigestion. Panama gains independence from Colombia while the U.S. negotiates for a canal to be built there.	Japan and Russia wage war. France and Britain become allies and sign a treaty. Roosevelt is re-elected president under the campaign promise "a square deal for all." The British make an arduous expedition to Tibet and sign a trade treaty there.
Rudyard Kipling publishes his *Just So Stories*. The Chinese custom of binding girls' feet is outlawed and denounced as barbaric. Beatrix Potter publishes *The Tale of Peter Rabbit*, part of the new wave in children's fiction. Women's fashions boast the 18-inch (45 cm) waist.	The Van Vorst sisters expose industrial sweatshops. A new pope, Pius X, is crowned in Rome. The first Tour de France, a bicycle race, is won by Maurice Garin; Boston beats Pittsburgh in baseball's first World Series. An auto race from Paris to Madrid is cancelled after spectators, unaccustomed to the high speeds (65 mph/104 kph) of the cars, wander onto the roadways and are killed or injured. Joseph Pulitzer establishes the first school of journalism at Columbia University. The world is introduced to Helen Keller through her book *The Story of My Life*.	The world-renowned World's Fair opens in St. Louis with the themes of education and American know-how. The ice-cream cone and automobile are among the displays. The United States wins the most medals at the Olympics in St. Louis, Missouri, held during the World's Fair. A woman in New York is arrested for smoking in public. The police say it is unseemly for women to smoke publicly. French sculptor Auguste Rodin exhibits *The Thinker* for the first time.
The vast Aswan Dam is opened on the Nile River in Egypt. It is built for agricultural purposes. Mount Pelée erupts, killing all but three inhabitants of Saint-Pierre, Martinique, in the Caribbean. One of the survivors was locked in jail at the time of the eruption. Mosquitoes are found to be the cause of yellow fever epidemics in Cuba.	The Wright Brothers make their historic flight near Kittyhawk. The Curies win the Nobel Prize for their work with radioactivity. Marie Curie is the first woman to receive the prize. Tom Fetch and M. C. Karrup drive across country in 51 days in a Packard Model F. Many people along their route have never seen a motorcar.	The Antarctic is explored by Captain Scott, the first person to reach the South Pole. Ivan Pavlov wins the Nobel Prize for his research on digestion. His famed study of response to unrelated stimuli becomes world renowned. The radio distress signal is established.

Time Line *(cont.)*

1905	1906	1907
Hundreds of unarmed protesters are massacred by police outside the czar's palace in Russia. Russia is struck by internal revolution over issues of labor and war. Meanwhile, Russia's navy, its last hope in its war against Japan, succumbs to Japan in the Tsushima Strait. Germany becomes allied with Russia in its attempt to enlarge its "sphere of influence."	President Roosevelt wins the Nobel Peace Prize for persuading Russia and Japan to end their war. Africans in Tanganyika rebel over foreign rule. They storm the German outposts, having been told by a "prophet" that the German bullets will turn to water. Hundreds of Africans are killed. France is granted a mandate over Morocco, allowing trading rights and the obligation to protect. Anti-Jewish riots spread through Russia.	Congo is purchased by Belgium in the wake of reports of devastating conditions there. Financier J. P. Morgan loans money to U.S. banks to curb a brewing economic panic. Mohandas Gandhi leads a peaceful resistance to South African racial discrimination. Rasputin gains influence over Czar Nicholas II. Suffragettes rally in an increasing effort to gain the vote for women.
Peter Pan, the play, opens in New York. It is written by James Barrie, who also wrote the book. In response to extraordinary public outcry over his famed character's death, Sir Arthur Conan Doyle brings Sherlock Holmes back to life in *The Return of Sherlock Holmes*. The rules for football are redefined, tempering what many consider to be a brutal game.	President Roosevelt's daughter Alice Lee is married in the White House. The public follows her romance with rapt attention. Major Alfred Dreyfus of France is honored with the Legion of Honor after having been cleared of 10-year-old charges that he spied for Germany.	Florence Nightingale is honored with the British Order of Merit for her nursing during wartime. The Plaza Hotel opens in New York and is heralded as the most beautiful hotel in the world. The first metered taxicabs are introduced. Due to increased traffic, the "traffic cop" is born. Roosevelt sends a fleet of 16 white battleships on a "Goodwill Cruise" around the world. Acclaimed lawyer Clarence Darrow successfully defends "Big Bill" Hayward against accusations of using violence to settle labor disputes.
Albert Einstein publishes papers on the nature of light and on his special theory of relativity. Air conditioning is introduced in a factory in North Carolina.	Natural disasters abound. Mount Vesuvius erupts, bringing death and destruction to southern Italy. A devastating earthquake strikes San Francisco; the quake and fires in the aftermath leave 250,000 homeless and thousands dead. Thousands die in Chilean earthquakes, and a typhoon leaves 10,000 people dead or missing in Hong Kong. A railroad tunnel through the Swiss Alps is opened, linking Switzerland and Italy. The project was begun one hundred years earlier by Napoleon.	The *Lusitania* breaks the transatlantic speed record. Advances in turbine engines produce speeds up to 35 knots. The electric washing machine is marketed.

Time Line *(cont.)*

	1908	1909
Politics and Economics	William Howard Taft is elected president. James S. Sherman is vice president. Two crises in the Balkans increase political unrest abroad and leave many fearing war in the future. More nations become allies in the face of the growing threat. The arms race between Britain and Germany escalates. The "Young Turks" of the Turkish Army oppose the sultan, causing mutiny and unrest. The sultan is forced to institute a constitution and a parliament. The U. S. Federal Bureau of Investigation is founded. The Chinese Empress Dowager dies after a long and treacherous rule. Assassination is suspected.	Serbia and Austria narrowly avoid conflict; however, the Balkans remain tense and war seems imminent. Rioting breaks out in Barcelona, halting work, trains, and streetcars. Religious buildings are burned as people blame the Spanish Catholic Church for their conditions. Francisco Ferrer is executed as the leader of the riots, although he was out of the country at the time. Prince Albert becomes the new king of Belgium. Turkey's sultan is deposed by the "Young Turks."
Social and Cultural	Sir Arthur Evans discovers the ancient city of Knossos in Crete. Roosevelt forms the National Conservation Commission to preserve forests and wildlife. The fifth modern Olympics are held in London before large crowds. There are competitions in 21 sports.	Immigration to the United States swells as millions come looking for a better life. The U.S. population reaches 92 million. The United States becomes multilingual in the face of mass immigration. Women's skirts shorten, with the hems of some dresses stopping above the ankle. Joan of Arc is declared "blessed" by Pope Pius X. This is a step along the road to her declaration as a saint.
Science and Technology	The first Ford Model T is produced. It seats two passengers, and costs $850. An earthquake and tidal wave strike Sicily. It is the worst earthquake known in European history. Due to the German-British arms race, great advances are made in battleship technology. Professor Ernest Rutherford wins the Nobel Prize for his theory of atomic transmutation. Railroad service begins under the Hudson River. The trip takes one-third the time of a ferry ride. The Wright Brothers are able to maintain flight for an hour.	Peary and Henson are the first to reach the North Pole. Pilot Louis Blériot becomes the first to fly across the English Channel. He flies at an average speed of 40 mph (64 kph). New York City becomes home to the world's largest skyscraper. It is 50 stories tall. The first skyscrapers were built in Chicago in 1890. Freud lectures on psychoanalysis and free association.

8

Using the Time Line

Use pages five through eight to create a visual display for your classroom. Follow the steps outlined below to assemble the time line as a bulletin board, and then choose from the suggested uses those that best suit your classroom needs.

Bulletin Board Assembly

Copy pages five through eight. Enlarge and/or color them, if desired. Tape the pages together to form a continuous time line, and attach it to a prepared bulletin board background or a classroom wall. (To make a reusable bulletin board, glue each page of the time line to oaktag. After the glue has dried, laminate the pages. Write on the laminated pages with dry–erase markers.)

Time Line

	1900	1901	1902	1903	1904	1905	1906	1907	1908	1909	
Politics and Economics	William McKinley is president. The Boer War is in its third year. Colonel Baden-Powell fools the Boers by having young boys carry wooden weapons along the perimeter of Mafeking. Thinking the town is well defended by British troops, the Boers keep away. The Boxer Rebellion ignites in China. The rebels believe that foxing and other exorcist protects them from ammunition. Hawaii is adopted as a territory of the United States. Eugene Debs announces his presidential candidacy under the newly established Social Democratic ticket. He is a supporter of laborers and a proponent of suffrage and equality.	President William McKinley is shot and killed. Vice President Theodore Roosevelt takes office, becoming the youngest president in history. Roosevelt fights against business monopolies and trusts. The six colonies of Australia unite to form a single nation. The United States begins to govern the Philippines. Future president William Taft is named governor. The Chinese government is forced to pay for the losses incurred during the Boxer Rebellion.	The Boer War finally draws to a close as the Boers surrender. Britain and Japan sign an agreement ensuring that Britain will not side with Russia in a dispute. A miners' strike in Pennsylvania leads to a shortage of coal throughout the nation.	King Alexander and Queen Draga of Serbia are assassinated by army officers. Turkish papers report the couple died of indigestion. Panama gains independence from Colombia while the U.S. negotiates for a canal to be built there.	Japan and Russia wage war. France and Britain become allies and sign a treaty. Roosevelt is re-elected president under the campaign promise "a square deal for all." The British make an arduous expedition to Tibet and sign a trade treaty there.	Hundreds of unarmed protesters are massacred by police outside the czar's palace in Russia. Russia is struck by internal revolution over issues of labor and war. Meanwhile, Russia's navy, its last hope in its war against Japan, succumbs to Japan in the Tsushima Strait. Germany becomes allied with Russia in its attempt to enlarge its "sphere of influence."	President Roosevelt wins the Nobel Peace Prize for persuading Russia and Japan to end their war. Africans in Tanganyika rebel over foreign rule. They storm the German outposts, having been led by a "prophet" that the German bullets will turn to water. Hundreds of Africans are killed. France is granted a mandate over Morocco, allowing trading rights and the obligation to protect. Anti-Jewish riots spread through Russia.	Congo is purchased by Belgium in the wake of reports of devastating conditions there. Financier J. P. Morgan loans money to U.S. banks to curb a brewing economic panic. Mohandas Gandhi leads a peaceful resistance to South Africa's racial discrimination. Rasputin gains influence over Czar Nicholas II. Suffragettes rally in an increasing effort to gain the vote for women.	William Howard Taft is elected president. James S. Sherman is vice president. Two crises in the Balkans increase political unrest abroad and leave many fearing war in the future. More nations become allies in the face of the growing threat. The arms race between Britain and Germany escalates. The "Young Turks" of the Turkish Army oppose the sultan, causing mutiny and unrest. The sultan is forced to institute a constitution and a parliament. The U. S. Federal Bureau of Investigation is founded. The Chinese Empress Dowager dies after a long and treacherous rule. Assassination is suspected.	Serbia and Austria narrowly avoid conflict; however, the Balkans remain tense and war seems imminent. Rioting breaks out in Barcelona, halting work, trains, and streetcars. Religious buildings are burned as people blame the Spanish Catholic Church for their conditions. Francisco Ferrer is executed as the leader of the riots, although he was out of the country at the time. Prince Albert becomes the new king of Belgium. Turkey's sultan is deposed by the "Young Turks."	Politics and Economics
Social and Cultural	France hosts the Summer Olympics in Paris. The first Davis Cup in tennis is won by Dwight Davis and Holcombe Ward. The Fifth Paris Exhibit amazes the world with its demonstration of technological advances such as electric lighting. Nations from around the world submit beautiful exhibits.	England's Queen Victoria dies, closing the long Victorian Age, which began in 1837. Andrew Carnegie announces his retirement and his plan to give away his fortune in acts of philanthropy. Booker T. Washington is invited to the White House. Author Leo Tolstoy, having written against the government and religion, is blamed for student riots in Russia. The Cossacks halt the riots. The U.S. wins the America's Cup.	Rudyard Kipling publishes his Just So Stories. The Chinese custom of binding girls' feet is outlawed and denounced as barbaric. Beatrix Potter publishes The Tale of Peter Rabbit, part of the new wave in children's fiction. Women's fashions boast the 18-inch (45 cm) waist.	The Wor West sisters expose industrial sweatshops. A new pope, Pius X, is crowned in Rome. The first Tour de France a bicycle race, is won by Maurice Garin. twelve beats Pittsburgh in baseball's first World Series. An auto race from Paris to Madrid is cancelled after operations, unaccustomed to the high speeds (65 mph/104 kph) of the cars, wander onto the roadways and are killed or injured. Joseph Pulitzer establishes the first school of journalism at Columbia University. The world is introduced to Helen Keller through her book The Story of My Life.	The world-renowned World's Fair opens in St. Louis with the themes of education and American know-how. The ice-cream cone and automobile are among the displays. This United States wins the most medals at the Olympics in St. Louis, Missouri, held during the World's Fair. A woman in New York is arrested for smoking in public. The police say it is unseemly for women to smoke publicly. French sculptor Auguste Rodin exhibits The Thinker for the first time.	Peter Pan, the play, opens in New York. It is written by James Barrie, who also wrote the book. In response to extraordinary public outcry over his famed character's death, Sir Arthur Conan Doyle brings Sherlock Holmes back to life in The Return of Sherlock Holmes. The rules for football are redefined, tempering what many consider to be a brutal game.	President Roosevelt's daughter Alice Lee is married in the White House. The public follows her romance with rapt attention. Major Alfred Dreyfus of France is honored with the Legion of Honor after having been cleared of 10-year-old charges that he spied for Germany.	Florence Nightingale is honored with the British Order of Merit for her nursing during wartime. The Plaza Hotel opens in New York and is heralded as the most beautiful hotel in the world. Sir Arthur Evans discovers the ancient city of Knossos in Crete. The first medieval tunicals are introduced. Due to increased traffic, the "traffic cop" is born. Major league baseball is dealt its first World Series loss.	The world's first medal for lifesaving is established. An earthquake and tidal wave strike Sicily. It is the worst earthquakes known to European history. Due to the German-British arms race, great advances are made in battleship technology. Professor Ernest Rutherford wins the Nobel Prize for his theory of atomic transmutation. Railroad service begins under the Hudson River. The trip takes one-third the time of a ferry ride. The Wright Brothers are able to maintain flight for an hour.	Immigration to the United States swells as millions come looking for a better life. The U.S. population reaches 92 million. The United States becomes multilingual in the face of mass immigration. Women's skirts shorten, with the hems of some dresses stopping above the ankle. Joan of Arc is declared "blessed" by Pope Pius X. This is a step along the road to her declaration as a saint.	Social and Cultural
				Roosevelt's first Model T is produced. It seats two passengers, and costs $850.					The first Ford Model T is produced. It seats two passengers, and costs $850. Roosevelt sends a fleet of 16 white battleships on a "Goodwill Cruise" around the world. Acclaimed lawyer Clarence Darrow successfully defends "Big Bill" Haywood against accusations of using violence to settle labor disputes.		
Science and Technology	Construction begins on the New York subway. The first Zeppelin airship takes flight. Motorcars powered by steam, electricity, and gasoline become more prevalent. By the end of the year, there are 8,000 cars on U.S. roads. Sigmund Freud's The Interpretation of Dreams is published.	A. E. Taylor is the first to go over Niagara Falls in a barrel. Guglielmo Marconi sends a wireless telegraphic signal across the Atlantic. Oil is discovered in Texas. A. C. Bostwick is the first to drive an automobile faster than a mile a minute.	The vast Aswan Dam is opened on the Nile River in Egypt. It is built for agricultural purposes. Mount Peléè erupts, killing all but three inhabitants of Saint-Pierre, Martinique, in the Caribbean. One of the survivors was locked in jail at the time of the eruption. Mosquitoes are found to be the cause of yellow fever epidemics in Cuba.	The Wright Brothers make their historic flight near Kittyhawk. The Curies win the Nobel Prize for their work with radioactivity. Marie Curie is the first woman to receive the prize. Tom Fetch and M. C. Karrup drive across country in 51 days in a Packard Model F. Many people along their route have never seen a motorcar.	The Antarctic is explored by Captain Scott, the first person to reach the South Pole. Ivan Pavlov wins the Nobel Prize for his research on digestion. His famed study of response to unrelated stimuli becomes world renowned. The radio distress signal is established.	Albert Einstein publishes papers on the nature of light and on his special theory of relativity. Air conditioning is introduced in a factory in North Carolina.	Natural disasters strike abroad. Mount Vesuvius erupts, bringing death and destruction to southern Italy. A devastating earthquake strikes San Francisco; the quake and fires in the aftermath leave 250,000 homeless and thousands dead. Thousands die in Chilean earthquakes, and a typhoon leaves 10,000 people dead or missing in Hong Kong. A railroad tunnel through the Swiss Alps is opened, linking Switzerland and Italy. The project was begun one hundred years earlier by Napoleon.	The Lusitania breaks the transatlantic speed record. Advances in turbine engines produce speeds up to 25 knots. The electric washing machine is marketed.		Peary and Henson are the first to reach the North Pole. Pilot Louis Blériot becomes the first to fly across the English Channel. He flies at an average speed of 40 mph (64 kph). New York City becomes home to the world's largest skyscraper. It is 50 stories tall. The first skyscrapers were built in Chicago in 1890. Freud lectures on psychoanalysis and free association.	Science and Technology

Suggested Uses

1. Use the time line to assess students' initial knowledge of the era. Construct a web to find out what they know about immigration or the Wright Brothers, for example. Find out what they would like to know. Plan your lessons accordingly.

2. Assign each group of students a specific year. As they research that year, let them add pictures, names, and events to the appropriate area of the time line.

3. Assign the students to find out what events were happening around the world during the first decade of the twentieth century. Tell them to add that information to the bottom of the time line.

4. After adding new names, places, and events to the time line, use the information gathered as a study guide for assessment. Base your quizzes and exams on those people, places, and events the students have studied.

5. After the time line has been on display for a few days, begin to quiz students about the people, places, and events named there. Call on one student at a time to stand so that he or she is facing away from the time line. Ask a question based on the information. *Variation:* Let the students compose the questions.

6. Use the time line as a springboard for a class discussion; for example, who was the most famous or most influential person of the first decade? How have the inventions of the first decade affected our lives today? How was life in the first decade similar to our lives today?

7. Divide the students into three groups, and assign each group a different area: politics/economics, society/culture, and science/technology. Have each group brainstorm important related people, places, and events that lived or occurred during the first decade; and then create a group mural depicting these important happenings and people. Get permission to decorate a hallway or tape several sheets of butcher paper together to make a giant canvas.

8. Assign groups of students to make specialized time lines—for example, a time line of revolution in Russia, a time line of the British-German arms race, or a time line of the history of flight.

Nineteen Hundreds Overview

- The dawn of the Golden Age came in 1900. People around the world looked for growth and opportunity in the new century, and many believed that their opportunities would come in America. Throughout the decade, millions of immigrants flocked to the United States in search of the "American dream." Some found it, while others lived their lives in pursuit of it; but always there remained the hope that hard work and determination would lead to a golden future.

- Queen Victoria died in 1901, marking the end of the Victorian Age. For 63 years she had been the symbol of the British Empire, of which the British said with pride, "The sun never sets on the Empire."

- Colonies and territories came with a price. Sometimes the citizens did not wish to be ruled by a country overseas, and turmoil ensued. The rush for power throughout Europe and Africa served, in part, as a catalyst for the great war of the next decade. The Boxer Rebellion, the Boer War, the Russo-Japanese War, and revolution in Russia added to the growing world turmoil, as did riots and rebellions in Spain, France, Turkey, the Gold Coast, and Tanganyika.

- As a result of the Spanish-American War, the United States gained control of the former Spanish colonies of Guam, Cuba, and Puerto Rico. A treaty with France and Great Britain created American Samoa in the South Pacific, and Hawaii was annexed.

- Oklahoma became a state in 1907, bringing the number of states to 46.

- Natural disasters struck around the globe. Mt. Pelée in the Caribbean and Mt. Vesuvius in Italy both erupted with tragic results. Italy, South America, and the United States all saw earthquakes that cost millions in damages and killed thousands.

- President McKinley was assassinated near the beginning of the decade. Theodore Roosevelt, the former Rough Rider and vice president, took the helm for most of the decade. Roosevelt fought hard to keep big business in check. He is perhaps most popularly remembered today for his namesake, the teddy bear.

- In 1907 Roosevelt sent "the Great White Fleet" of American naval ships around the world to demonstrate American strength.

- The International Ladies Garment Workers Union began in 1900. The Industrial Workers of the World, a militant labor union sometimes called "Wobblies," was founded in 1905.

- Industry and invention revolutionized the world. Earlier inventions such as the telephone and the electric light came into widespread use. Automobiles began to replace bicycles and horse-drawn vehicles, and wireless communications connected the world in new ways.

- Lyman Frank Baum published *The Wonderful Wizard of Oz* in 1900. The first of fourteen books about Oz, it has become a children's classic.

- Cinema moved from vaudeville houses to small theaters called nickelodeons. *The Great Train Robbery* set the pace for melodramas, and Georges Melies of France experimented with special effects in *A Trip to the Moon*. Film censorship began in 1909.

- The Wright brothers brought flight to the world with their successful ride at Kittyhawk, North Carolina.

- The age of the automobile came into full swing as Henry Ford introduced the mass-produced Model T.

- At the close of the decade, Peary and Henson became the first people to reach the North Pole, decreasing the amount of unexplored land on the planet. Little did the average person think that the close of the new century would bring exploration beyond the planet and throughout the galaxy.

Introducing the Nineteen Hundreds

On this page you will find some interesting ways to introduce the 1900s to students. Keep in mind that these are suggestions only, and it is not necessary to use all of them. Your project selections should be based on students needs, interests, and objectives.

1. **Sing Along:** Learn about popular songs of the first decade of the twentieth century. Teach some to the class or create a demonstration of the songs and their origins. Look to Americana songbooks as your sources.

2. **Fashions:** Slim waists, above-the-ankle hemlines, and pompadour hairstyles came into vogue in the first decade. Have students find pictures of clothing from this era. Excellent sources are the paper doll books published by Dover Publishing of New York.

3. **Art Work:** Display artwork either of the time (such as Picasso, Cézanne, Cassatt, or Gauguin) or that which reflects life during the time. Assign students to create their own artwork reflective of the first decade.

4. **Hats:** Most people wore hats in public during the early twentieth century. Allow students to become haberdashers by creating their own hats representing the styles of the era.

5. **Electricity:** Create a class display showing the evolution of electrically run products with origins in the first decade. This may be as simple as a then-and-now bulletin board.

6. **Read Aloud:** Read aloud from classic books of the time such as James Barrie's *Peter Pan,* Beatrix Potter's *The Tale of Peter Rabbit,* L. Frank Baum's *The Wizard of Oz,* Sir Arthur Conan Doyle's *The Return of Sherlock Holmes,* and Rudyard Kipling's *Just So Stories.* You might also choose such sophisticated writings as those of Sigmund Freud in his *Interpretation of Dreams* or the controversial work of Kate Chopin in her shocking-for-the-time novel, *The Awakening* (published in 1899).

7. **Guest Speaker:** Contact local colleges, universities, museums, and historic societies for potential speakers who are experts on the era. Have students prepare questions to ask the speaker about the time.

8. **Interview:** Have students research famous people from the first decade of the twentieth century and dress as these people. Allow the class to interview them in character.

9. **Inventions:** The first 10 years of the new century were filled with exciting new inventions. Research some of those inventions and discuss how they changed the lives of people around the world. Some inventions to consider are aircraft, automobiles, and electrically operated machinery (see #5 above, also).

10. **Melting Pot:** Many people still consider the United States to be a great melting pot of world cultures. The first decade of the century certainly saw a great deal of immigration and, therefore, the introduction of new cultures, languages, and ways of life into the mainstream of society. Brainstorm some of those cultures and their contributions to American culture as a whole. Discuss immigration of the time and immigration today.

11. **Golden Age:** Direct the students to research what clothing was popular with young people at the turn of the century, and then specify a day on which they should come to school in such clothes. Serve them ice-cream cones in traditional cornucopias (waffle cones). Study Latin. Read by oil or gas lamp, and then switch to a single electric bulb and compare the two. Read the "funny papers." View the Ziegfeld Follies sequence from the film *Easter Parade.* Play cricket.

Discussing the Nineteen Hundreds

Create student interest with a lively discussion. Suggested topics and some methods for implementing them follow:

Turn of the Century: The dawn of the 21st century can be compared and contrasted to the dawn of the 20th. How are they alike? How are they different? What feelings do they evoke?

Electricity: Electricity has had a profound influence on life in the 20th century. Discuss the changes students perceive to have begun in the first decade and how those changes have affected the ensuing years. Also discuss what life might be like today without the invention of electricity.

Warring World: Great political upheaval began in the first decade, culminating in World War I in the 1910s and World War II in the 1940s. Discuss the state of the world today and the possibilities for World War III. Also discuss what it may have been like to live from 1900 through 1909 with the perpetual threat of war and revolution.

Teddy Bear: The teddy bear was named for President Theodore Roosevelt. Ask the students to consider the idea of a toy named for them (individually or as a group). What might the toy be called and why?

Unions: Many labor unions began to take shape in the first decade of the 20th century to combat unhealthy, unsafe, and unfair conditions in the factories and workplaces of the previous years. Discuss the differences such unions may have made, considering the pros and cons of the issue.

Let's Go to the Movies: Cinema moved from vaudeville houses to small theaters, or nickelodeons, during the first decade. What effect has cinema had on life and culture over the years?

On the Move: The ability to get from one place to another changed dramatically during the early nineteen hundreds. In terms of transportation, discuss the differences in time and convenience from the end of the 19th century to the beginning of the 20th. Then discuss those same differences from the beginning of the twentieth century to its conclusion.

Exploration: A new wave of exploration occurred during the first decade, including Scott's study of the Antarctic and Peary and Henson's trip to the North Pole. Compare the pole explorations of the 1900s with the world explorations hundreds of years prior (Columbus, Magellan, etc.) and the space explorations later in the century.

Assassination of a President

The first president of the new decade was William McKinley, a Civil War veteran who was instrumental in bringing the United States into position as a world power. He is also noted for his efforts to minimize big business.

McKinley believed that government needed to deal with the problem of industrial consolidation in which businesses in the same industry joined together to create large, monopolizing businesses. On September 5, 1901, President McKinley spoke at the Pan American Exposition in Buffalo, New York, on this issue as well as on the issue of tariffs. He had modified his earlier views in support of protective tariffs for businesses to support free commerce through reciprocal trade agreements. These are agreements between countries to reduce each other's tariffs mutually. McKinley believed that these agreements would help to increase "the outlets for our increasing production." He declared, "The period of exclusiveness is past."

Certainly not everyone was in support of McKinley's new ideas. Many did not want government restrictions and regulations on business. One such man, Leon F. Czolgosz, an anarchist, was among the crowd at the Pan American Exposition. On September 6, the day after McKinley spoke, Czolgosz and others attended a reception held by the president at the exhibition's Temple of Music. Czolgosz carried a revolver covered with a handkerchief wrapped about his hand like a bandage. As President McKinley approached him and reached out to shake his hand, Czolgosz reached out his left hand as if to shake and fired twice with the gun held in his right. The first bullet ricocheted off McKinley's jacket button, but the second pierced his stomach.

President McKinley was rushed to the hospital for surgery. He continued to live for eight days; however, his wound became infected and gangrene set in. Though at first it was thought that he would recover, on September 14, 1901, President McKinley died.

At the time of the shooting, Vice President Theodore Roosevelt was hiking in the Adirondack Mountains of New York. He was told that the president would probably recover. However, word was sent later that McKinley was near death. Roosevelt rushed back, but by the time he reached Buffalo on the fourteenth, the president was dead. Roosevelt was sworn into office on the same day.

Leon Czolgosz was tried for murder and eventually executed by electrocution.

Suggested Activities

Research and Compare: Find out about other assassinations and assassination attempts in the history of the presidency. Compare them, particularly the motives.

Modern Medicine: Early in the twentieth century, death through infection was much more common than it is today. Research to determine what medical advances have come about to help reduce the risks.

Assassin: Find out more about the life of Leon Czolgosz and his motive for killing President McKinley.

Modern Travel: Compare the time it took Roosevelt to get from the Adirondacks to Buffalo to the time it would take the vice president to make that trip today. What accounts for the time difference?

Eugene Debs and the Social Democratic Party

Times were changing rapidly at the turn of the century. People were beginning to think in unprecedented ways. Laborers started looking for social and political equity, women organized to procure the right to vote, and a growing number of voices gathered to call for equality among the races. Such voices were not the majority nor were they even heard in some areas, but speak they did, and some louder than others. One such voice was that of Eugene Victor Debs.

Born in Terre Haute, Indiana, in 1855, Eugene Debs did a variety of work before his political career began. In 1885 he served his first political office in the Indiana State legislature. Then, in 1893, he organized and became president of the American Railway Union, leading an important labor strike on the railroad in 1894. In the fallout of the strike, Debs was arrested and jailed.

While in jail, Debs was introduced to the concept of Socialism, a political and economic doctrine that calls for ownership of exploitable resources and all means of production by the central government, not individuals, thereby (ideally) creating total economic equality for everyone. The American Socialist editor Victor Berger gave Debs *Das Kapital* by Karl Marx, as well as other Socialist books and information. Debs liked what he read, and in 1898 he organized the Social Democratic Party of America. In 1900 he became the party's first candidate for the office of president of the United States. Debs ran again as the party's candidate in 1904, 1908, 1912, and 1920. Never successful in his attempts to gain the presidency, Debs' popularity and ideas spread nonetheless. He became a renowned lecturer and organizer of the Socialist movement in America, gaining the respect of people from many walks of life and with typically opposite viewpoints. His passion and his dreams for equality caused quite a stir; and although he was never president, his campaigns did have certain effects on the outcomes of elections and on the overall changes within the nation.

During World War I, Debs, due to his pacifist beliefs, was sentenced to a term of 10 years in prison; however, his sentence was commuted, and he was released in 1921. In the election of 1920 (while in prison), Debs received nearly one million popular votes.

Suggested Activities

Other Socialist Leaders: Eugene Debs was not the only prominent Socialist of the time. Other important figures included Karl Kautsky, Rosa Luxemburg, and Eduard Bernstein. Each of these held somewhat different views regarding Socialism. They also differed from the views of Marx himself. Research their perspectives, and create a chart that shows the similarities and differences.

Socialism Today: While no countries today are purely Socialist, Socialist parties do exist throughout the world. Research to find the state of Socialism in the United States as well as elsewhere in the world. How is it similar to and different from the Socialism espoused by Eugene Debs?

Debate: Divide into teams, and debate the pros and cons of Socialism or Socialism vs. Capitalism.

Labor Unions: Labor unions gained in strength and power throughout the nineteen hundreds. Research to learn about important unions of that time and those with significant power today. How have the roles of labor unions changed over time?

Pennsylvania Coal Strike

Throughout the nineteenth century, laborers with disputes against their employers had little recourse for solutions. Sometimes they would strike, but often those strikes ended in bloodshed and with little advancement being made. In the 1880s and 1890s, laborers frequently worked 12 hours per day, seven days per week, in harsh and dangerous conditions. Environments were frequently harmful, but if workers became ill or injured, they had no sick leave or worker's compensation—no work, no pay.

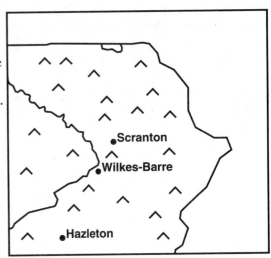

Due to the vast number of industrial laborers in the area, Pennsylvania became a significant player in the United States labor movement. More and more, laborers banded together to instigate change. Anthracite mine workers found a need to unionize after a series of continuing problems, so they formed the United Mine Workers, which included both skilled workers and immigrant laborers. Anthracite coal—which is coal with the highest carbon content and heating ability—is found in the United States, almost exclusively in the areas surrounding Scranton and Wilkes-Barre, Pennsylvania. At the time the United Mine Workers formed, this area was supplying most of the coal to the entire country.

In 1902 the union decided to aggressively seek a 20 percent pay increase, a nine-hour workday, and safer conditions for laborers. The only method for negotiation was to strike, which had always proved dangerous and bloody in the past. For five months, from May through October, members of the union refused to work. With winter approaching, the nation began to panic. Its coal supply was extremely limited, and the people did not have many other options for acquiring coal. However, President Theodore Roosevelt stepped in and appointed an investigative commission, while at the same time threatening to send U.S. troops to work the mines. He encouraged financier J. P. Morgan to negotiate with the mine owners, and eventually a settlement was reached through arbitration. The workers received their nine-hour day and a pay increase of ten-percent; however, the owners would not recognize the union. Nonetheless, a solution had been reached without the customary level of violence.

This settlement became a precedent for nonviolent arbitration between laborers and management. Future disputes would begin to use the results of the Pennsylvania coal strike as a model on which to base their own arbitration, thereby decreasing the violence and bloodshed normally associated with such disputes. The coal strike also served as another model: the extent to which a U.S. president might intervene in business operations. Although Roosevelt had seriously extended his powers, popular opinion remained strongly in support of him and his ability to find solutions.

Suggested Activities

Mining: As a class, learn how coal is mined. Compare the differences between mining in the early 1900s and mining today. Study the dangers for coal miners in 1902.

Investigate: Bring coal samples into the classroom. Conduct scientific experiments on the coal to learn about its composition and properties.

Suffragettes

Throughout the nineteenth century, groups of women organized and demonstrated to reform education, establish rights to property, and provide opportunities for certain previously unattainable professions (such as medicine) for women. By the time the twentieth century dawned, they had begun to focus their goals on the right to vote, also known as *suffrage*. These women reformers became known as *suffragettes*.

There was strong resistance to the movement throughout the country and, in fact, throughout the Western world. Women everywhere were fighting for the right to vote, but tradition, prejudice, and in some, a sense of moral righteousness proved difficult to combat. However, the suffragettes persisted. They themselves sometimes disagreed on tactics; however, they strongly believed that all methods of reform should be strictly legal so as to combat any suggestion that women are emotionally volatile and therefore incompetent to vote.

The National American Woman Suffrage Association (NAWSA) was highly active at this time. It held conventions, waged state-by-state campaigns, and distributed literature to bring about change. Suffragettes followed the example of women in Britain who were fighting for the vote and held parades and outdoor speeches on a regular basis. Eventually, the cause realized that it needed to appeal to two factions of women, both the social reformers and those seeking equal rights. The social reformers realized that they needed the vote to bring about change, and college-educated, working, and career-minded women were natural supporters of equal rights. The union of the two groups proved successful. Little by little, individual states began to give the vote to women, though it would not be until the close of another decade that the United States Constitution was amended to give women the vote.

Suggested Activities

Influential Women: Research the lives and influences of Alice Paul, Lady Astor, Lucy Stone, Henry Blackwell, Susan B. Anthony, and Elizabeth Cady Stanton on the suffrage movement.

Voting and the Sexes: Examine the differences in voting results when only males vote, when only females vote, and when both sexes vote. Conduct class votes on various subjects. Have all voters mark their ballots "M" for male or "F" for female, or provide differently colored ballots to each sex. Discuss the results and differences, if any. Consider a wide variety of topics for voting.

NAWSA: The NAWSA was formed from the combination of the National Woman Suffrage Association (NWSA) and the American Woman Suffrage Association (AWSA). Research to find out more about these organizations and their dynamic founders. How did the two differ from one another, and why did they decide to join forces?

Hawaii

Throughout the nineteenth century, Hawaii's sugar cane industry grew into large money-making ventures. Businesses founded by descendants of American missionaries and whalers increasingly wished to dismantle the Hawaiian monarchy and to make Hawaii a territory of the United States, thereby increasing profits. However, King David Kalakaua and his sister Queen Liliuokalani (*Lē-lē´-ŏo-ō-kă-lă´-nē*), who ruled Hawaii at the end of the nineteenth century, hoped to retain Hawaii for native Hawaiians and preserve their own culture.

Queen Liliuokalani

In 1893 a handful of American and European residents with the help of American marines and sailors overthrew the last monarch, Queen Liliuokalani. These individuals formed the Republic of Hawaii in 1894 and elected Sanford B. Dole, the U.S. Consul, as its first and only president. The American business executives continued to push for United States rule (under which they would be exempt from paying the high McKinley tariff imposed on foreign products shipped to the continental United States). In 1898 Hawaii was annexed as a possession of the United States; and finally, despite some Hawaiian opposition, Hawaii became a United States territory on June 14, 1900. As such, all residents became U.S. citizens. Dole was appointed by President McKinley as the first governor of the new territory.

Suggested Activities

Statehood: Hawaii did not become a state until 1959, making it the youngest of all states in the Union. Find out the facts about how Hawaii's statehood came to be.

Dole Company: Find out about the Dole Company and its origins and operations in Hawaii.

Pineapple: At the beginning of the twentieth century, pineapple joined sugar as an important Hawaiian crop. Research this plant and its place in the history and economy of Hawaii.

Hula: Traditional hula dances tell the stories of Hawaiian history and its important people. The dance was banned by early missionaries. King Kalakaua worked to preserve and restore the hula dance as part of Hawaiian culture. Learn a simple traditional hula or create one to tell a story.

Music: Queen Liliuokalani, the sister of King Kalakaua, composed a number of songs, including "Aloha Oe," which means "farewell to you." If possible, listen to this song in Hawaiian and English.

William McKinley

25th President, 1897–1901

Vice Presidents: Garret A. Hobart (1897–1899); Theodore Roosevelt (1901)

Born: January 29, 1843, in Niles, Ohio

Died: September 14, 1901

Party: Republican

Parents: William and Nancy McKinley

First Lady: Ida Saxton

Children: Katherine (A second daughter died in infancy.)

Education: Allegheny College (did not graduate); law school in Albany, NY

Famous Firsts:

- McKinley was the first president of the new century.

Achievements:

- McKinley and his secretary, George Cortelyou, developed new procedures for interacting with the press, including the distribution of press releases and the provision of space in the White House where reporters could work. McKinley made himself accessible to the press on a regular basis.

- McKinley is credited with strengthening the power of the presidency. He is also noted for bringing the United States into position as a world power.

- While under intense enemy assault during the battle of Antietam, 19-year-old McKinley took food to his regiment, earning him honors for bravery under fire.

- McKinley oversaw the Gold Standard Act of 1900, making only gold, not silver, exchangeable for money in the U.S.

- Under his leadership, the U.S. took possession of Guam, Puerto Rico, the Philippines, Hawaii, and part of American Samoa.

Interesting Facts:

- McKinley was devoted to his wife and very protective of her because she was an invalid and an epileptic. He was never far from her or away from her for more than a few hours. He often left meetings just to check on her. His devotion to her was such that when he was shot, he called out to his secretary, "My wife—be careful, Cortelyou, how you tell her!"

- Those who knew McKinley considered him a very kind and gentle man. For example, when he thought that he would need to declare war on Spain, it is reported that he broke into sobs. Also, after he was shot, he asked the bystanders in attendance not to harm Czolgosz, the man who attacked him.

- McKinley was the first man in his town of Poland, Ohio, to volunteer to fight in the Civil War.

- The 23rd Ohio Infantry, to which McKinley belonged during the War, was commanded by future president Rutherford B. Hayes.

- Through the 1870s and 1880s, McKinley served seven terms in Congress. He then served as governor of Ohio.

- The president was noted as a gifted public speaker and was generally popular and well liked.

18

Theodore Roosevelt

26th President, 1901–1909

Vice President: Charles W. Fairbanks (1905–1909)

Born: October 27, 1858, in New York City

Died: January 6, 1919

Party: Republican

Parents: Theodore Roosevelt and Martha Bulloch

First Lady: Edith Kermit Carow (first wife, Alice Hathaway Lee, died in 1884)

Children: Alice; Theodore, Jr.; Kermit; Ethel Carow; Archibald Bulloch; Quentin

Nickname: Teddy or T. R. (Teedie as a child)

Education: Harvard University

Famous Firsts:

- Roosevelt was the youngest man (age 42) ever to become president.
- He was the first American to receive the Nobel Peace Prize.
- He was the first president to ride in an automobile and to fly in an airplane.
- Roosevelt was the first president to travel to a foreign country (Panama) while in office.
- Roosevelt coined the term "muckraker," signifying writers who sought to expose corruption.

Achievements:

- Roosevelt fought for construction of the Panama Canal.
- He helped bring an end to the Russo-Japanese War.
- Roosevelt was known as a "trust buster," breaking up the power of large corporations.
- Roosevelt established five national parks and added about 150 million acres to the national forests. He also established the United States Forest Service, set aside 18 sites as national monuments, and created the first bird and game preserves.
- In 1902, the White House was remodeled and enlarged.

Interesting Facts:

- After a cartoonist drew Roosevelt with a bear cub, the "teddy bear" became popular.
- The Rough Riders, commanded by Roosevelt during the Spanish-American War, were comprised primarily of former college athletes and Western cowboys.
- He was a distant relation of future president Franklin Delano Roosevelt.
- Frequent illnesses, including asthma, were catalysts for young Theodore to build his strength and lead an extremely active and strenuous life. He regularly worked out in a gymnasium, rode horses, swam, hunted, hiked, and boxed.
- Roosevelt's foreign policy, "Speak softly and carry a big stick," was a West African proverb.
- His first wife and his mother died on the same day, February 14, 1884.
- Roosevelt frequently swam across the icy Potomac in the wintertime.
- Roosevelt's is one of four faces carved on Mt. Rushmore.

William Howard Taft

27th President, 1909–1913

Vice President: James S. Sherman
Born: September 15, 1857, in Cincinnati, Ohio
Died: March 8, 1930
Party: Republican
Parents: Alphonso Taft and Louise Maria Torrey
First Lady: Helen Herron
Children: Robert, Helen, Charles
Nickname: Big Bill
Education: Yale College and Cincinnati Law School

Famous Firsts:

- Taft was the first president to serve on the Supreme Court.
- He was the first to protect federal lands on which oil had been found.
- He bought the first cars used at the White House, and he built the first garage for their storage.
- Taft was the first president to throw out the first ball on the opening day of the baseball season.
- Always large, Taft was the heaviest president ever, weighing 332 pounds at his inauguration.
- Under President McKinley's appointment, he became the first commissioner of the Philippines, a holding the United States won from Spain in 1900.
- He was the first president to be buried at Arlington National Cemetery. The only other president buried there is John F. Kennedy.

Achievements:

- He took steps toward establishing a federal budget by having his cabinet members submit reports of their needs. It was estimated that he saved the nation $42 million in 1910.
- Taft actualized many of Roosevelt's programs by working them into law during his presidency.
- He was very successful in protecting federal lands set aside for conservation. In fact, he was even more successful than Teddy Roosevelt, whose name is usually linked with conservation.
- Taft oversaw twice as many prosecutions under the Sherman Anti-Trust Act as did Roosevelt. Most impressively, Taft succeeded in breaking up the Standard Oil Company monopoly.
- The Sixteenth and Seventeenth Amendments were passed while Taft was in office.
- New Mexico and Arizona became states during his presidency.
- After the presidency, Taft became a law professor at Yale, the president of the American Bar Association, chairman of the National War Labor Board, and Chief Justice of the United States.

Interesting Facts:

- Taft never really wanted to be president. His desire was to serve on the Supreme Court.
- Due to Taft's size, a new bathtub had to be placed in the White House. It could hold four average-sized adults.
- Taft was often criticized for playing golf, a rich man's game. However, he played while conducting business with important leaders, a fact that the newspapers never reported.
- The president was most criticized because of his differences with Teddy Roosevelt. Although Roosevelt had handpicked Taft as his successor, he later changed his mind when he saw that Taft was more conservative than he liked. Taft had also changed members of Roosevelt's old cabinet, although Roosevelt had promised them they could keep their positions. Taft was deeply hurt by Roosevelt's rejection. Roosevelt had been his mentor. The strife between the two split the Republican party and made the way easier for a Democratic president in the next election.

Now a Word from the President

Theodore Roosevelt is remembered today as one of the greatest presidents in American history. His unique character and the many changes he made to government and society are remembered with nearly as much passion as are those of Washington and Lincoln. He is perhaps best known, however, for his legacy of words. Phrases from his speeches and campaigns have become part of the national vocabulary.

Read the phrases below. After each, write what you think Roosevelt meant. Then do some research to find where or how it originated and what it really means.

Roosevelt's Words	What I Think	Origin and What It Means
Speak softly and carry a big stick.		
muckraker		
square deal		
one of the governing class		
Rough Riders		
Bully!		
Fear God and take your own part.		
grape juice diplomacy		

Teddy Bear

When a cartoonist drew a picture of President Theodore Roosevelt holding a bear, the imagination of the nation caught fire and the teddy bear was born. It became an instant success; and as a testament to its popularity, there is hardly a child born today who is not given a teddy bear of his or her own.

Other presidents of the twentieth century have also inspired interest in commercial products, such as the increase in jellybean sales during the presidency of Ronald Reagan or peanuts while Jimmy Carter was in office.

For this assignment, you will need to do a little research. Choose a twentieth-century president, and write about an item that gained popularity as a direct result of its connection with that president. Explain what the item is and how it is connected to the president. Also, explain whether or not the item's popularity has continued since the end of the presidency.

22

Press Release

Under the presidency of William McKinley, the press first got a foothold into the regular operations of the White House. A press room was made available for the journalists, the president often met there with them, and press releases were prepared on a regular basis to update the media on current events.

Choose a significant event that occurred during McKinley's, Roosevelt's, or Taft's presidency. In the space below, write a press release that provides the most significant information about the event. Be sure to write the release in such a way as to support the president's perspective. (In modern terms this is called "putting a spin" on the information. It means that the writer presents the news with a subtle bias in his or her favor, attempting to sway the readers' perspectives.)

White House Press Release

Date:_____

Election Facts and Figures

	Election of 1896	Election of 1900
Democrats	William Jennings Bryan of Nebraska, a prominent orator, was the Democratic nominee with Arthur Sewall, a wealthy Maine shipbuilder, as his running mate.	William Jennings Bryan was once again the Democratic nominee; Adlai E. Stevenson, vice president under Grover Cleveland, was his running mate.
Republicans	William McKinley, the 1892 candidate, ran with Garret A. Hobart of New Jersey.	President McKinley ran for a second term, this time with Theodore Roosevelt, a war hero and New York governor, as his running mate.
Issues	The primary issue was whether or not silver should be allowed to back American currency. McKinley supported free silver while in Congress; then as a candidate, he supported the gold standard.	Free silver was again an issue as well as big business and illegal monopolies (trusts).
Slogans	"Free silver" and "gold standard" were the words most often heard in this election. McKinley said, "Good money never made hard times."	"A Full Dinner Pail" was the successful slogan used by the McKinley/Roosevelt ticket.
Results	McKinley took 271 electoral votes to Bryan's 176. McKinley had more than 7 million popular votes, and Bryan had more than 6.5 million.	McKinley's electoral vote was 292 against Bryan's 155; the popular vote was similar to the previous election, with slightly more for McKinley than for Bryan.

24

Election Facts and Figures *(cont.)*

	Election of 1904	Election of 1908
Democrats	Judge Alton B. Parker of the New York Supreme Court was the Democratic nominee with Henry G. Davis of West Virginia as his running mate.	William Jennings Bryan of Nebraska made his third attempt at the presidency on the Democratic ticket. John W. Kern, a Democratic leader from Indiana, was his running mate.
Republicans	President Roosevelt (president since 1901 when McKinley died) was unanimously nominated by his party, and Senator Charles W. Fairbanks of Indiana became his running mate.	William Howard Taft was Theodore Roosevelt's choice for his successor. James S. Sherman, a congressman from New York, was his running mate.
Issues	Parker argued that the office of the president was usurping authority. Roosevelt called for support of his "square deal" policies which involved social reform.	Government corruption and unfair business practices were major issues. Bryan was a supporter of income tax, prohibition, and women's suffrage. All his causes eventually became law.
Slogans	Roosevelt's campaign centered around the phrase "A square deal for all."	Taft campaigned as "Bill."
Results	Roosevelt won by a larger popular vote margin than any previous president. He took more than 7.5 million votes (336 electoral), and Parker took just over 5 million (140 electoral).	Taft took 321 electoral votes to Bryan's 162. Taft's popular vote exceeded 7.6 million, while Bryan's was just over 6.4 million.

More About the Elections

Here are some ways to use the Election Facts and Figures on pages 24 and 25. Select those activities and projects which best suit your classroom needs.

1. Prepare a classroom chart with four different sections, each marked with a vice president's name from the 1900s. Pair the students. Allow each pair to select a vice president's name. (You may wish to randomly assign names.) Instruct the pairs to find out more about the men nominated for vice president: where they were born, their childhoods and schooling, their political backgrounds, what became of them once they were out of office, and so forth. Compile all the information gathered onto your prepared chart.

2. President Roosevelt won by a wide margin in the campaign of 1904. Research as a class to determine the reasons why Roosevelt won so handily.

3. Percentages of electoral votes do not always seem to reflect the percentages of popular votes. Have the students study the electoral system to determine how it works. They can then take sides in a debate about this system of electing a president.

4. Roosevelt first became president due to the death of President McKinley—Roosevelt was not elected to the office. Learn about other presidents through the years who first gained office in ways other than direct election.

5. "Free silver" and the "gold standard" became important terms in elections at the turn of the century. Do some research to determine what these terms mean, why they were important, and the effects they had on the elections.

6. In the election of 1896, big business contributed the unprecedented amount of 3.5 million dollars to McKinley's campaign. McKinley was able to use this money to alter public opinion about his competitor, William Jennings Bryan, and to sway the voters in his favor. Research the facts to determine how this was possible. Also consider how campaign spending has affected elections over time. Debate the pros and cons of spending big dollars during any campaign.

7. Throughout the first decade of the 20th century, Republicans held the presidency. What affect did this have on the nation? Compare this period of time to other times in American history that have been dominated by the Republicans or Democrats over a space of 10 or more years.

8. Extend the information provided on pages 24 and 25 with other facts and figures. For example, find out how many popular votes the candidates garnered in their respective elections. Make a chart comparing the figures. See page 27 for some math problems that use these figures.

9. McKinley's presidency was enormously effective in connecting the United States to the world, bringing it from isolation to a global position. Research to find why this was so and how it happened.

10. Bryan attempted to gain the presidency three times during the 1900s. Looking into the facts of history, discuss the reasons why he remained unsuccessful. Then, let student teams take on the job of Bryan's campaign manager, designing a campaign strategy (for one of the elections) that the team feels would win Bryan the position. Let the teams share their strategies with the class.

Election Math

In the chart below, you will find the number of electoral votes and popular votes for each presidential election from 1896 to 1908. Use this chart to answer the questions that follow. Show your work.

Year	Candidate	Electoral Vote	Popular Vote
1896	Bryan	176	6,509,052
	McKinley	271	7,111,607
1900	Bryan	155	6,356,734
	McKinley	292	7,218,491
1904	Parker	140	5,084,491
	Roosevelt	336	7,628,834
1908	Bryan	162	6,412,294
	Taft	321	7,675,320

1. How many more electoral votes were there in 1908 than in 1900?

2. How many popular votes were there altogether in 1904?

3. How many total electoral votes were cast in all four elections combined?

4. Using the figure from problem #3, what is the average number of electoral votes per election? (Round the answer so it is not a decimal.)

5. Using the answer from problem #4, which actual number of electoral votes (total from one election) comes closest to the average number?

6. What is the combined number of popular votes that Bryan received in his three elections?

7. What percentage of popular votes did Roosevelt receive in 1904? (Round the answer.)

8. What percentage of electoral votes did Roosevelt receive in 1904? (Round the answer.)

The Changing World

During the nineteen hundreds, major political shifts and skirmishes occurred throughout the world. Here are some of the most significant:

Year	Event
1900	• Hawaii becomes a U.S. territory.
	• Britain and South Africa remain at war as the Boers fight foreign rule.
	• China sees the Boxer Rebellion.
1901	• The United States governs the Philippines.
	• Australia becomes a commonwealth and a part of the British Empire.
	• President McKinley is assassinated.
	• Peace of Peking ends the Boxer Rebellion.
1902	• Britain, France, and Germany seek "spheres of influence," allies and political holdings to increase their power.
	• Britain wins the Boer War, and a treaty is signed.
	• The Triple Alliance among Germany, Austria, and Italy is renewed for six years.
1903	• Panama gains independence.
	• Serbia's monarchs are assassinated.
	• Pope Pius X is crowned. He has great political influence.
1904	• France and Britain strike a treaty, an *entente cordiale.*
	• Japan and Russia go to war.
	• Britain and Tibet sign a trade treaty.
1905	• Russia and Germany become allies.
	• There is revolution in Russia.
	• Japan wins the war against Russia.
1906	• Morocco becomes a French mandate.
	• There is rebellion in Tanganyika against foreign rule.
1907	• The Belgian government purchases the Congo Free State.
	• There are riots in France.
	• Indian immigrants protest in South Africa.
	• New Zealand becomes a British dominion.
	• Britain, France, and Russia sign the Triple Entente.
1908	• Turkey is forced to designate a parliament and a constitution.
	• Crisis in the Balkans nearly forces war.
	• An arms race between Britain and Germany escalates. War seems imminent.
1909	• Serbia and Austria narrowly avoid war.
	• There are riots in Spain.
	• Young Turks take over Turkey from the sultan.
	• U.S. population swells to 92 million after a decade of enormous immigration.

Suggested Activities

Research: Instruct student teams to research one of the events above to explain its impact on the immediate area it affected and on the world as a whole. Have students keep in mind the event's relevance to World War I, which occurred in the next decade.

Cartography: Find or draw maps of the world's national boundaries circa 1900, 1909, and in the present day. Compare the changes.

28

The British Empire

In the 1900s, it was said that "the sun never set on the British Empire." This meant that it was daylight on at least one British colony at all times. That was how vast the British Empire was.

Beginning in the late sixteenth century, Britain chartered commercial ships and acquired lands for the sake of sugar, tobacco, the slave trade, and missionary work. The nation began to acquire lands and holdings around the world until the late nineteenth and early twentieth centuries, when it had reached the height of its political power. Large sections of Asia, Africa, and North America were in its control.

As the chart on page 28 shows, Britain's attempts to gain "spheres of influence" did not end with the new century. War and domination escalated, and with the domination came rebellion. The mounting disputes had their culmination in the next decade as Britain found itself embroiled in the first world war.

Suggested Activity

Piece of the Empire: This map shows the British Empire circa 1909. Choosing one of the nation's areas of domination, research to find how Britain acquired that particular holding and what happened to Britain's power there later in the century. Finally, tell how things stand today between Britain and the area you have chosen.

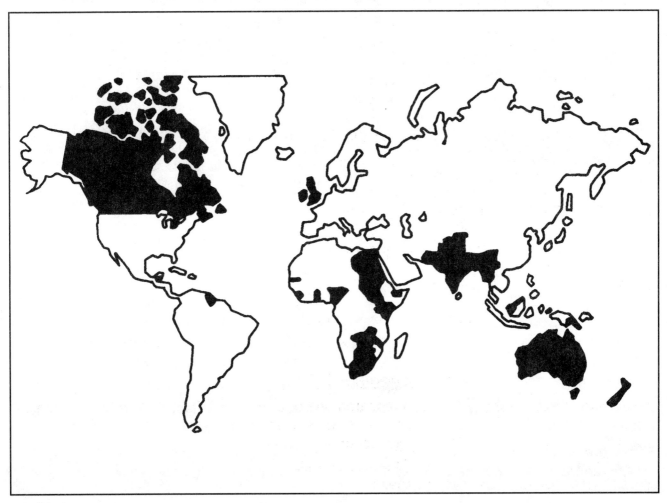

German Power

At the dawn of the twentieth century, Germany was the most populated and prosperous country in Europe. Its art, music, philosophy, science, and technological advances were heralded internationally. However, its naval expansion and the military's inclusion in most German affairs made the world uneasy. Germany seemed to place strong emphasis on building a powerful military.

When Germany involved itself in the Balkan crisis and various Middle Eastern affairs, the world became suspicious and went on guard. The Triple Alliance that Germany formed with Austria-Hungary and Italy served to divide Europe, resulting in a similar treaty among France, Britain, and Russia.

At the center of German machinations was William II (also called) Kaiser Wilhelm, emperor of Germany and king of Prussia. His policies would lead directly to the First World War in the coming decade.

Kaiser Wilhelm was the son of Prince Frederick William (later the German emperor, Frederick III) and Princess Victoria, eldest daughter of Britain's Queen Victoria. Wilhelm became emperor in 1888 upon his father's death. Frederick III had served as emperor for only three months.

Prior to Kaiser Wilhelm's leadership, Germany had grown extensively under the guidance of Prince Otto von Bismarck, Germany's chancellor (appointed by Wilhelm's grandfather, William I). However, William II chose to dismiss Bismarck in 1890, and he himself undertook the management of all domestic and foreign policies. Most significantly, he changed Germany's primary occupation from agriculture to industry. With the growth of industrialization came labor disputes and the rise of the Social Democratic Party. (See page 14.) This party would grow to become the largest in the empire and would eventually be part of William's undoing.

William believed in expansion, and he put Germany's resources fully behind the expansion of its colonies, commerce, and navy. Meanwhile, although asserting that Germany was a friend to Britain, William's policies forced Britain, France, and Russia into an alliance that would serve as a basis for division in World War I. Similarly, while espousing friendship with Russia, he supported Austria-Hungary in the Balkans, thereby alienating the Russians. Ironically, he saw his own nation's involvement in the Triple Alliance with Austria-Hungary and Italy as a deterrent to war; time would show it to be a factor in eventual outbreak of war.

After World War I, William was forced to abdicate his throne, and he lived his remaining years in exile and seclusion. However, he did live long enough to see Germany's military power rise again. He died in 1941, prior to Germany's final fall from military power.

Suggested Activities

Map It: Learn about Germany's international empire in the 1900s. Draw and label a map to show the nation and its holdings.

Chancellor: Find out about the life of Otto von Bismarck and the effect he had on Germany's rise to international power.

Who's the Boss?: Different nations use different systems of leadership and terminology. Investigate the meanings and occupations of the following: emperor, chancellor, and king/queen.

Russian Revolution and Japanese Victory

At the turn of the century, Russia was a place of unrest and mounting revolutionary ideas. Marxism was on the rise, and from it sprang a revolutionary leader, Vladimir Ulyanov. Today, the world remembers Ulyanov by the name he took in 1901 to confuse the police: Lenin.

Vladimir Lenin

Lenin was a leader in the Russian Social Democratic Party formed in 1898. (See page 14.) The party split in 1903 over membership disputes. The minority, *Mensheviks*, wanted few restrictions on party membership and favored democratic practices. The majority, of which Lenin was the leader, became known as the *Bolsheviks*. They urged limited party membership and rule of the proletariat (workers) by trained professionals.

At the time, Czar Nicholas II was in power in Russia, but there was a growing lack of support for his rule. People wanted more freedom, higher wages, and better representation. On Sunday, January 22, 1905, Father George Gapon, a Russian Orthodox priest, organized a group of 200,000 to make a peaceful march on the Winter Palace in St. Petersburg (later Leningrad, after Lenin). The marchers were unarmed, but government troops were ordered to fire into the crowd. Hundreds were killed or wounded. The conflict became known as Bloody Sunday, and it added fuel to the mounting revolutionary fire.

At the same time, conflict between Russia and Japan was mounting. They both had interests in the same lands, particularly Korea and Manchuria. In 1902 England made an alliance with Japan in protest of the Russians. In 1904 Japan attacked a Russian fleet, unprovoked and without warning. They followed this with a declaration of war on Russia. The Japanese led the war, but with the help of American President Theodore Roosevelt, the fighting ceased after a little more than a year. A peace treaty was signed in 1905. The treaty gave the Liaodong Peninsula, Korea, the southern half of Sakhalin Island, and railway rights in Manchuria to Japan. This territory established Japan as a world power.

In Russia, the unrest grew, partly as a result of the Russo-Japanese war. Strikes broke out, and military and peasant groups revolted. Nicholas agreed to establish a fully elected lawmaking body, grant the right to vote, establish freedom of speech, and pardon all political exiles, including Lenin; but the protests continued. Lenin returned to Russia in November of 1905 and called for a full revolt. Russia seemed on a course that could not be halted or altered. A mass strike began in December, and soon it developed into a full revolution. By the end of the month, the revolution had been crushed, but time would show that the revolution of 1905 was, as Lenin declared, merely a "general rehearsal (for) the victory" of the revolution that was to come.

Suggested Activities

History: Follow the path begun by the Revolution of 1905, tracing it through the full revolution that brought communism to Russia through most of the twentieth century. Also learn about Lenin's role in the later revolution and what finally became of the Bolshevik leader.

Application and Projection: Have the students write about the American Revolution of 1776, altering history to show an American loss. How might that have changed history? What do they think might have happened?

The French Connection

France was no stranger to world power by the 1900s. Under the leadership of Napoleon a century before, France had gained extensive holdings and expanded in control. However, over the years it lost a great deal of ground. Germany was quickly exceeding the population and economic power of France, and after 1871, France found itself without allies.

Otto von Bismarck of Germany encouraged France to follow Germany's lead and look to colonialism for expansion. France did, and soon it had established significant colonial holdings in Africa and Asia. The French Empire became second in size only to the British Empire.

In the late nineteenth century, Russia and Germany began to lose favor with one another. This proved to be France's opportunity, and it was especially useful since Russia's position allowed France to have an ally along Germany's eastern front. By 1894 France and Russia agreed to support each other militarily should there be any dispute between either of them and Germany or Austria-Hungary. Britain joined allegiance with France a decade later when Germany's growing power forced them both to seek allies and support. After Britain and Russia came to terms with their former differences, France, Britain, and Russia signed the Triple Entente, which put them in direct opposition to the Triple Alliance of Germany, Italy, and Austria-Hungary. From 1904 through 1914, France was under an almost perpetual threat of war. The great world war did eventually break out in 1914.

France—like Britain, Germany, Russia, and Japan—attempted to gain power, strength, and control throughout the 1900s. The result for every nation was financial ruin, countless lives lost, and geographic devastation.

——— Suggested Activity ———

Cartography: Using an atlas and the map of France below, add the following countries: Great Britain, Germany, Switzerland, Monaco, Italy, Austria, Hungary, Belgium, and Spain. Then explain the geographic significance of Germany, Italy, and Austria-Hungary in terms of economic and political power.

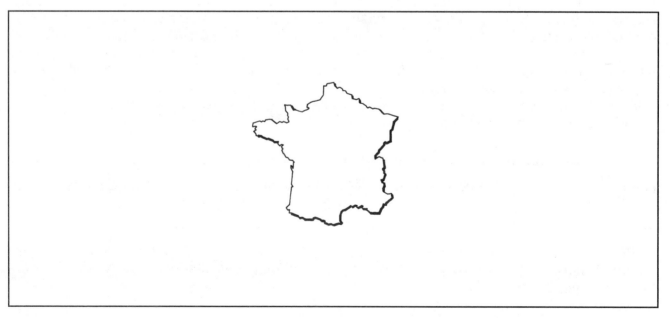

The American Dream

The United States is largely composed of people whose ancestors were at one time immigrants to the country. The first immigrants came primarily from Western Europe for reasons of political oppression, religious persecution, and internal strife. In the mid-nineteenth century, immigrants hailed mainly from Great Britain, Ireland, and western Germany. From 1860 to 1890, people from those same countries continued to come to the United States, along with many from the Scandinavian nations. Finally, from 1890 through 1910, the percentage of immigrants from those nations dropped to one-third, while the remaining two-thirds came from Austria, Italy, Russia, and Hungary. From 1905 to 1914, the United States saw an average of a million or more immigrants per year.

If one studies the events and circumstances of the immigrant nations during the years that saw extensive population shifts, it is easy to determine why people left their familiar surroundings to seek the American dream. The political upheaval and race for power that blew through many European nations during the 1900s had a significant impact on immigration to the United States. Likewise, reports of greater opportunity in the U.S. made the move all the more enticing.

In the United States itself, people were not always pleased to receive the immigrants. Many laborers feared they would lose their jobs to the immigrants who were willing to work for much less money. Also, when the volume of immigrants from southern and eastern Europe started to arrive, their unfamiliar languages and customs disturbed American citizens who were not particularly open to the unfamiliar—even if they themselves were immigrants at one time.

However, despite the dubious welcome and the fears surrounding new beginnings, millions of immigrants continued to come into the country throughout the first decade of the twentieth century. Mass immigration only took a sharp decline when World War I broke out, but after the war the numbers rose again. Volumes of immigration continue to this day, although the people who come to the country are primarily from other areas of the world, such as Mexico and Haiti.

Wherever it is from which people hail, there are always important reasons why people are willing to leave their homelands and to start a new life. These reasons are at the heart of the American dream.

Suggested Activity

Why?: Choose a nation from which there was mass immigration to the United States from 1900 through 1909. Research to find the reasons why so many chose to leave their homelands. How do those reasons affect the "spheres of influence" various European nations were trying to attain during that period?

The Golden Age

People of the nineteenth century generally looked to the twentieth century to make their dreams come true. The turn of the century was seen as an opportunity for fulfillment of bright promises made through the growth and industrialization of the 1800s. It was hoped that the year 1900 and beyond would bring the realization of possibilities. For many, it was looked to as the dawning of a Golden Age.

The majority of the previous century had been lived in the Victorian Era, but now was the time for change. The new century would complete the millennium, and many felt that anything was possible. Progress and prosperity were around the corner, and more than anything, people of the Western world were certain that peace was here to stay.

However, as the next decade proved, peace was not permanent, and many more changes were to come. Even so, the new century did bring amazing advances in technology, medicine, international relations, and more. Here are a few that came in the years 1900–1909:

Planck and Einstein: The decade opened in 1900 with Max Planck's proposition of a quantum theory which revolutionized the field of physics. In 1905, Albert Einstein began to make a name for himself with his publication of a paper on relativity. The work of both men would eventually earn them Nobel prizes in the coming years.

Photography: In 1900 the Kodak Brownie box camera was introduced, making home photography accessible and simple.

Radio: The first transatlantic radio transmission came in 1901. The first voice and music radio broadcast in the United States came about in 1906.

Flight: In December of 1903, Wilbur and Orville Wright's first plane flew for the first time. By 1908 they had closed a contract with the U.S. Department of War for the first military airplane. The first commercial airline followed in 1909.

Automobiles: The Ford Motor Company was founded in 1903. In the next decade, cars would become commonplace.

Pierre and Marie Curie: This couple discovered radium and polonium in 1898 and shared the Nobel Peace Prize for Physics in 1903.

Subways: The incredible New York subway opened its first section in 1904. New York's subway system is still world renowned. New York also awed the world with the Williamsburg Bridge in 1903 and the Manhattan Bridge in 1909.

North Pole: The impossible happened: two men, Robert E. Peary and Matthew Henson, reached the North Pole in 1909. It seemed there was nowhere in the world where man could not go.

Suggested Activity

Research: Find out more about any of the advances listed above. What led to their development? What improvements or changes have been made to them since?

Gandhi

Mohandas Gandhi is considered by many to be the greatest spiritual and political leader of the early twentieth century. He is also considered by the people of India to be the father of their nation. There he is called the Mahatma, or the Great Soul.

Gandhi lived his life in a search for truth, and he believed that truth could be found only through compassion and tolerance of others. Further, he believed that truthful solutions to problems could always be found if one persevered.

Mohandas Gandhi

Gandhi was born on October 2, 1869, in Porbandar, India. Shy and serious, he married his wife, Kasturba, at the age of thirteen through an arranged marriage. The couple had four children. Gandhi studied law in London and returned to India in 1891 to practice. Two years later, he went to South Africa to do legal work but met with great discrimination, as did most Indians despite the fact that they were British subjects and South Africa was under British rule. Although he was assigned to South Africa for only one year, he remained for 21 years to fight discrimination. He developed a method of using passive resistance and non-cooperation to effect social change. This method, which he called *Satyagraha* (truth and firmness) was based in part on the teachings of Christ and the works of Leo Tolstoy and Henry David Thoreau. He stressed the need for honor; the way people behaved was of the utmost importance.

After his years in South Africa, Gandhi returned to India where he quickly became the leader of the Indian nationalist movement. He led the people in nonviolent resistance and protest to British rule. Often he fasted in protest, and he was jailed several times; but no matter what, he persevered.

Eventually, after many years, India did gain its independence. However, the nation split in two, and Hindus, Muslims, and other groups fought against one another. Gandhi turned his nonviolent protests to the cause of uniting all groups in harmony. Ironically, while on the way to a prayer meeting, an assassin's bullet killed this man of peace just twelve days after religious leaders had agreed to stop fighting.

About Gandhi, Albert Einstein is quoted as having said, "Generations to come will scarcely believe that such a one as this walked the earth in flesh and blood."

Suggested Activities

British Empire: In the early twentieth century, the British Empire held lands around the world, among them India and South Africa. Find out more about this period of time and what eventually happened to the vast empire.

Animal Rights: Gandhi believed that it was morally wrong to kill animals for food or clothing. Discuss your views on this subject.

Marriage: In Gandhi's culture and among his caste (socio-economic level in India), arranged marriage was common, and the age of thirteen for marriage was not considered young. Research to learn about marriage in other parts of the world in the early 1900's as well as the practices of marriage around the world today. Chart the comparisons.

Social Leaders: Compare Gandhi to other leaders who have urged nonviolent protest, most notably Martin Luther King, Jr.

Carry Nation

There are not many who have come to represent a righteous and strident call for morality in quite the way Carry Nation did. Her name has become synonymous with moral action, although certainly not everyone of her time agreed with her idea of morality.

Carry Nation was born Carry Amelia Moore in Kentucky in 1846. At 20, she married an alcoholic, Dr. Charles Gloyd, who died shortly after they were married. After ten years of supporting herself by teaching and renting out rooms, she married a lawyer and minister named David Nation. She became devoutly religious at this time and professed that she saw visions. Nation was convinced that she was divinely protected and divinely chosen. A fire in 1889 that burned much of her town but left her property untouched increased her belief. So did her name—Carry A. Nation. She felt quite certain it was a message to her from Providence.

Carry Nation

In 1889 Mr. and Mrs. Nation moved to Kansas. There was a law in Kansas at this time banning the sale of liquor, but it was not enforced. Carry Nation took it upon herself to enforce it. In 1890, she began to pray outside saloons, and later, through the first decade of the twentieth century, she began to smash them. When she is pictured today, she is still seen carrying her Bible and wielding her hatchet, her tools of destruction.

One might not think that one woman could make much difference; however, the nearly six-foot (183 cm) Carry Nation and her hatchet did extensive damage and closed the saloons in her town, as well as many others throughout Kansas. Although she was often arrested for disturbing the peace, she continued to carry on her personal crusade.

Nation was also opposed to other things she found morally corrupt, such as the use of tobacco and immodest dress in women. Many felt her sense of righteousness was justified, so she developed quite a following of imitators and fans who admired her courage. However, many others were angered by her intolerant actions and dismissed her for her inappropriate and outrageous behavior. In 1901 Nation's husband divorced her on the grounds of desertion.

Suggested Activities

Discussion: Discuss the following questions:

- Are there any causes you feel so passionately about that you would feel justified in taking matters into your own hands?

- What social activists today might you compare to Carry Nation? How do you feel about their work?

Write: Have the students write on the following topic: Carry Nation felt called upon to lead her crusade. What do you feel called upon to do in life?

Prohibition: The crusade of Carry Nation was, in part, instrumental in bringing about Prohibition in 1919. Research Prohibition in the United States and what happened to the amendment banning the sale of alcohol throughout the country.

The Nobel Prize

Alfred Bernhard Nobel (1833–1896) is the Swedish chemist and industrialist who invented dynamite. The sale of dynamite and other explosives made Nobel a very wealthy man. In his will, he set aside nine million dollars. The interest earned by this money was to be used to present cash awards each year in each of five categories that benefited humanity: physics, chemistry, physiology or medicine; literature of an idealistic nature; and the most effective work toward international peace. The prizes were first presented in 1901. In 1969 a sixth prize for economic science was added by the Bank of Sweden. By the late twentieth century, the value of each of the prizes had reached approximately $900,000.

Use encyclopedias and other reference materials to match the names of the Nobel Prize winners below with their achievements.

1. _____ Mother Teresa

2. _____ Pierre and Marie Curie

3. _____ Ivan Pavlov

4. _____ Martin Luther King, Jr.

5. _____ George Bernard Shaw

6. _____ Rudyard Kipling

7. _____ Toni Morrison

8. _____ Max Planck

9. _____ Jane Addams

10. _____ Albert Schweitzer

a. work on the physiology of digestion

b. stories, novels, and poems

c. stating the quantum theory of energy

d. work with Women's International League for Peace and Freedom

e. discovery of radioactivity and studies of uranium

f. humanitarian work in Africa

g. novels

h. plays

i. aiding India's poor

j. leading nonviolent civil rights demonstrations in the U.S.

The Graduate

Helen Keller

Helen Adams Keller was born normal and healthy in 1880, but at age one and a half she suffered what the doctor called "acute congestion of the stomach and brain." The illness destroyed her sight and hearing. For nearly five years afterwards, Keller was almost completely cut off from the rest of the world, unable to speak and communicating only through giggles and choked screams.

At the advice of Alexander Graham Bell, Keller's father wrote to the Perkins Institution for the Blind, in Boston. Just before Keller turned seven, Anne Mansfield Sullivan arrived to undertake her teaching. Together they developed a way to communicate with Sullivan manually into Keller's hand. Once the girl understood the method, her learning was rapid. Within three years, Keller was a fluent reader and writer of Braille, the alphabet of the blind.

At age 10, Keller took lessons from a teacher of the deaf to learn how to speak. At 16, she went to preparatory school and continued her studies at Radcliffe College. Anne Sullivan attended classes with her as her interpreter. In 1904 the impossible happened. The blind and deaf young woman, once entirely unable to communicate, graduated from college—with honors.

Helen Keller went on to be a noted author (her books have been translated into over 50 languages) and lecturer. Communication became her gift to the world. She worked for the remainder of her life to help the blind and deaf, doing such things as starting the Helen Keller Endowment Fund and working with World War II soldiers who had been blinded in battle.

Some of Keller's books include *The Story of My Life* (1902), *Optimism* (1903), *The World I Live In* (1908), and *Teacher* (1955) which is the story of Anne Sullivan. Helen Keller's early life has been immortalized in the award-winning play *The Miracle Worker* (1959) and the motion picture of the same name.

Suggested Activities

Braille: Below you will find the Braille alphabet as it appears visually, along with four words made with their own dot codes. In reality, the dots are raised indentations on paper. Use the system of dots as you see it to write a message. Have a classmate translate your work.

A	B	C	D	E	F	G	H	I	J

K	L	M	N	O	P	Q	R	S	T

U	V	W	X	Y	Z	and	of	the	with

College: Helen Keller was able to attend and graduate from college, but it is unlikely that she would have been able to do so without the help of Anne Sullivan. Do some investigating to find out what help is available in colleges today for people with special needs.

Boy Scouts

In 1907, Robert Baden-Powell of Britain began the Boy Scouts movement by organizing a camp for boys. The following year, he published the first Boy Scout manual. One year later, an American businessman, William D. Boyce, was traveling in England when he became lost in a London fog. A British Boy Scout helped him find his way. Boyce, impressed by the Scout's actions, brought the organization to the United States. It has grown by leaps and bounds ever since, spreading to more than 130 countries with over 24 million members.

The Boy Scouts is an organization that was founded to teach young men leadership and good citizenship. Service to God, country, and others is intrinsic to the Boy Scout way of life. The Scouting organization teaches its members to learn by doing; therefore, they are given hands-on, cooperative experiences in the areas of camping, first aid, outdoor cooking, swimming, woodworking, and more.

Boy Scouts take an oath which is a promise to do their duty. They also pledge to follow the Scout Law, which has twelve points. The Law states that a Scout is as follows:

• trustworthy	• courteous	• thrifty
• loyal	• kind	• brave
• helpful	• obedient	• clean
• friendly	• cheerful	• reverent

Scouts earn badges and promotions in their troops as they grow and accomplish the work set before them to learn and do. Today, any boy from six to twenty years of age may be a Scout member; girls from fourteen to twenty may join the Explorers, a division of the Boy Scouts.

Suggested Activities

Scout Oath: Each Boy Scout swears the Boy Scout Oath. It reads as follows:

> *On my honor, I will do my best:*
>
> *To do my duty to God and my country, and to obey the Scout Law.*
>
> *To help other people at all times.*
>
> *To keep myself physically strong, mentally awake, and morally straight.*

Write your own oath that states the way in which you believe you should live your life.

Scout Law: The 12 points of the Scout Law are listed above. Write each of the points on a sheet of paper. Next to each, write how well you honor that part of the Law in your own life. Also write what points you would include in a law you wrote for yourself.

Carnegie's Philanthropy

Born in Scotland in 1835, Andrew Carnegie moved with his family to the United States when he was twelve. He taught himself to send telegraph messages, and this led to a position with the Pennsylvania Railroad. Carnegie advanced quickly through the company, and he began to invest his earnings in iron.

In his mid-thirties, Carnegie traveled to Europe. It was there that he took an interest in steel, and this became the basis of his great fortune. Over the years, he built a huge steel company, that withstood hard times and competition to become the industry's leader. His talents as a salesman and his business savvy helped his company grow by leaps and bounds. When he sold his company in 1901 to businessman J. P. Morgan for $480 million dollars, he was heralded as the richest man in the world.

After his retirement from the steel industry, Carnegie chose to spend his remaining years working for the common good. Although he did not believe in charity, he did believe that it was essential for wealthy people to help others help

Andrew Carnegie

themselves. He began many such helping organizations and funds for those who worked in education or who worked to help others. It is estimated that he donated approximately $350 million dollars to various causes. Carnegie built the world-famous Carnegie Hall in New York City, and perhaps most notably, he was instrumental in the development of more than 2,500 public libraries around the world.

When Carnegie died in 1919, he left behind a legacy of philanthropy that has seldom been matched. He was truly one of the great businessmen and philanthropists of the century.

Suggested Activities

$350 Million: Have each student make a list of the ways in which they would spend $350 million dollars on philanthropic causes.

Helping Others: Take on a class project that involves helping others to help themselves. This might be tutoring, teaching a skill, or helping a small business get up and running by handling some appropriate tasks.

Carnegie Hall: Many performers look to Carnegie Hall as being the ultimate place to perform. Trace its history and the entertainers who have performed there. Ask the students why they think it has come to be so famous.

Booker T. Washington

Booker T. Washington

Booker T. Washington, born a slave, became arguably the most influential black leader of his time. He urged education, primarily through the Tuskegee Normal and Industrial Institute (now Tuskegee University) which he founded in 1881, as well as economic advancement for blacks. Perhaps most significantly, he became a trusted advisor to Presidents Roosevelt and Taft and influenced the appointments of several blacks to positions in the federal government.

Born in 1856, Booker Taliaferro Washington lived as a slave in Hales Ford, Virginia, until emancipation in 1865. His family then moved to West Virginia, where Washington labored in the mines and salt furnaces while studying at the Hampton Institute, an industrial school for blacks. Eventually, Washington became a teacher at the school; he then took many of its theories and practices and put them into the framework of the new school he developed in Tuskegee. Specific trades were taught at the school, such as carpentry, mechanics, and teaching. In order to support the school, Washington became an expert fund raiser. The school began to draw attention and became a model of industrial education.

Washington had very specific reasons why his school would teach trades as opposed to a traditional college education. He believed that the way out of poverty for blacks was hard work through trades so that they could purchase property; and then, once they were economically secure landowners, political and civil rights would follow. Washington urged blacks to focus on education and economic growth and to stop focusing their demands on equal rights. At the same time, he urged whites to give blacks better jobs.

Washington spoke publicly on many occasions. Perhaps his most famous speech was the "Atlanta Compromise." In it, Washington accepted inequality for blacks in exchange for economic growth. However, this does not mean that Washington did not support equal rights. He carefully avoided publicly supporting issues that would displease prominent Southern whites, but at the same time he secretly financed lawsuits that fought to increase black rights and oppose segregation. He also funded and ran a number of black newspapers.

Despite Washington's prominence, there were backlashes and some opposition, particularly through W. E. B. Du Bois (page 42), who felt that Washington was surrendering rights for economic gain and that higher education was vital for black advancement. Du Bois also objected to Washington's control of so many newspapers, believing that such control allowed only Washington's opinions to be heard. By 1910 Washington's influence was on the decline.

Suggested Activities

Read: Read *Up from Slavery: An Autobiography* (Corner House, 1971). It was first published in 1901, and in it, Washington explains his life as well as his theories.

Tuskegee: Research the Tuskegee Institute and its history. Find out about the curriculum and attendance today.

Washington vs. Du Bois: Discuss the views of these two black leaders. Do you agree with Washington's or Du Bois' point of view?

Advisor: Washington was one of the first black advisors to a president, paving the way for future blacks not only to advise but to hold the office of president, as well. Investigate the roles of advisors to the presidency over time. How influential can they be? How influential was Washington? Should advisors have influence in the first place?

W. E. B. Du Bois and the NAACP

Like Booker T. Washington, William Edward Burghardt Du Bois was a prominent black leader early in the twentieth century. However, his beliefs and perspectives differed radically from Washington's.

Du Bois was born in Massachusetts in 1868, and he lived for nearly one hundred years. He graduated from Fisk University in 1888, and in 1895 he became the first black to earn a Ph.D. from Harvard University. He then became a professor at Atlanta University as well as a renowned author, particularly for *The Souls of Black Folk* (Fawcett, 1961), a collection of essays and sketches published in 1903.

W. E. B. Du Bois

Booker T. Washington and W. E. B. Du Bois shared the same goal—advancement and equality for blacks; however, while Washington urged hard work in place of demands for equality, Du Bois believed that blacks must be relentless in speaking out against discrimination and fighting prejudice. Du Bois supported college education, while Washington put his power behind vocational training and financial security.

In order to fight racial discrimination, Du Bois founded the Niagara Movement in 1905. The next step came in 1909 when he and approximately 60 other blacks and whites founded the National Association for the Advancement of Colored People (NAACP). The NAACP works tirelessly to end discrimination through legal action and legislation, and it attempts to reduce hunger and poverty for people of color as well. In its first 30 years, it also worked to halt violence against blacks, particularly through the passage and enforcement of anti-lynching laws. Just after its inception, the NAACP began to produce *Crisis*, a magazine filled with stories of blacks who achieved success. For 24 years, Du Bois was its editor.

Today, the NAACP is headquartered in Baltimore with a legislative bureau in Washington, D.C. Out of the NAACP has grown the NAACP Legal Defense and Educational Fund in New York City. The Fund has been independent since 1957.

After many years of working with the NAACP, Du Bois grew dissatisfied and frustrated by the slow progress toward racial equality in society and the law. In the two years prior to his death, Du Bois joined the Communist party and moved to Ghana where he died in 1963.

Suggested Activities

Find Out More: To learn more about the NAACP, read *History and Achievement of the NAACP* by Jacqueline L. Harris (Watts, 1992). You can also write directly to the NAACP at 485 Mt. Hope Drive, Baltimore, Maryland 21215.

Read: If your library has access to them, locate and read old copies of *Crisis*. As a class, write your own modern issue of the magazine.

Communism: Discuss why you think Communism held appeal for Du Bois.

Mary McLeod Bethune

Mary McLeod Bethune was born in 1875 in Mayesville, South Carolina, the sixteenth of seventeen children. Former slaves, Mary's parents now worked as sharecroppers. To earn additional income, her mother also cooked for the people who once owned her.

Bethune was extremely interested in education but little opportunity was available to her. There were no schools open to African-American children where she lived; however, when she was eleven, a missionary school at which she could receive instruction opened in a neighboring town. Although the school was five miles away, Bethune walked there every day for the three months of the year it was open to her. (During the remaining months, children were expected to work the farms.) At home, Bethune taught what she had learned to her siblings.

Bethune eventually received a scholarship and attended Scotia Seminary. After finishing her studies, she became the head of a missionary school in Florida. She taught school in Florida and Georgia from 1897 to 1903. In Florida, at the age of 22, she married fellow teacher Albert Bethune.

As Mary Bethune learned of the railroads being built and the mass migration of African-American people to previously unsettled areas, she grew concerned for the black children who would move away and have no place to attend school. On October 3, 1903, she chose to open her own school, the Daytona Normal and Industrial Institute for Negro Girls. Within two years, Mary Bethune had 250 students attending her school.

Always an advocate for the betterment of African-American people, Bethune also opened a hospital for blacks and started the Better Boys Club, a social place for young people that would provide alternatives to poolrooms and other "undesirable places." When her school merged with the established Cookman Institute for Boys, Bethune-Cookman College was born.

In the coming decades, Bethune would continue as a strong advocate for the rights and advancement of African Americans. She organized the National Council of Negro Women; served as the director of Negro Affairs in the National Youth Administration; and was vice president of the Urban League, president of the Association of Colored People, and vice president of the National Association for the Advancement of Colored People. As a member of Franklin D. Roosevelt's "Black Cabinet," she joined professionals and advisors who promoted black issues.

Until her death in May of 1955, Bethune worked tirelessly for the causes of education and equality for all. Throughout her long life, she made a tremendous difference for millions of people.

Suggested Activities

Motto: The motto for Bethune's first school was "Enter to learn, depart to serve." Instruct students to write what they think this means. Then discuss their ideas.

Education: Today in America, education through high school is free and available to all young people. Learn about the history of education in the United States. How have laws and opportunities changed over time?

Eleanor Roosevelt: Mary McLeod Bethune and Eleanor Roosevelt were very close friends. Learn about their friendship and the effects Bethune had on FDR's presidency.

World Series

At the turn of the century, baseball was capturing the hearts and spirits of the American people. To capitalize on this growing passion, the first post-season baseball series, called the World Series, was played in 1903 between the leader of the American League (Boston) and the leader of the National League (Pittsburgh). Boston took the series five games to three. The World Series has been played every year since, except 1904 (due to an internal dispute) and 1994 (due to a player strike). Eventually, the event became a best-of-seven series; therefore, to win the championship today, a team needs four victories.

Baseball and its heroes have been immortalized in poetry, plays, and more than 400 songs. "Take Me Out to the Ball Game," written in 1908, is perhaps the most enduring and well-known of these baseball songs. American children throughout the nation generally grow up with a familiarity of baseball. Even young children can usually recognize the equipment of the game.

How well do you really know baseball? Complete the activity below to find out.

——— Suggested Activity ———

Positions:
Using the diagram, write the names of the positions played next to their corresponding letters.

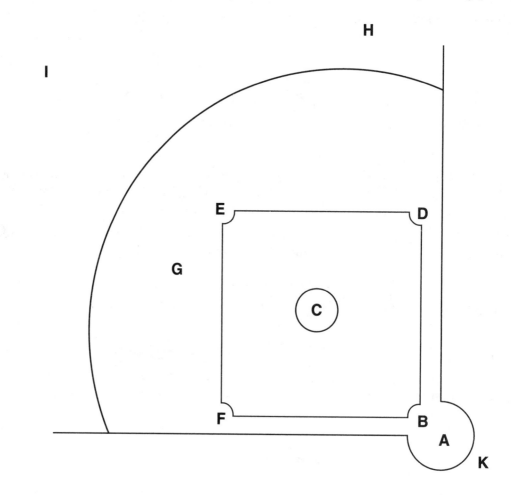

Davis Cup

In the world of international men's tennis, the Davis Cup is the most prized team trophy. It began with an intercollegiate and doubles tennis champion named Dwight Filley Davis, who, in 1900, donated the silver cup. Competition in his name began that year. Each year since (excepting 1901, 1910, and the years of the two world wars), the Davis Cup has been in continuous competition.

To earn the Davis Cup, the top 16 qualifying nations compete in a single elimination tournament. A separate tournament is played among the nonqualifying nations divided into four zones. The leader of each zone advances to Davis Cup competition in the following year, replacing the losing teams of the previous Cup competition.

When play for the Cup began, the competitors were teams from America and the British Isles. By World War I, six more nations had joined, and by 1984, there were a total of 62 nations in competition. Up until 1927, only America, Great Britain, and Australasia (a combined team of Australia and New Zealand) had won the trophy, but France won in 1927 as well as in the next six tournaments. However, France has not won since, and Great Britain has not won since 1937. From then until 1974, the cup went to either America or Australia (now in solitary competition). South Africa became the victor in 1974 but only through default. At the time, many nations objected to South African politics. In the final round of competition, South Africa and India were set to play for the championship, but India refused, despite the fact that its win would mean the first win for an Asian nation. India's default led to South Africa's victory.

Today, the sport of tennis is filled with professionals, but in earlier years it was not. In fact, professionals were barred from Davis Cup play until 1968.

Suggested Activities

Winners: Research to find the winners of each of the Davis Cup competitions. Make mathematical graphs comparing the leading nations, runners-up, scores, and more.

War Disruptions: War and conflicts have often put a halt to international athletic competitions. Have a class discussion considering why this is so, if such disruptions are necessary, and what might be done about them if they should happen in the future.

Playing Tennis: Allow the class to study the basic rules of tennis and to play the game. Take some physical education time learning to serve, return the ball, volley, and more.

Default: In 1974, South Africa topped India in the Davis Cup competition by default. Research to find the facts behind this unusual result.

Politics: Dwight Davis went on to become a successful lawyer, lieutenant-colonel in the army, secretary of war under President Calvin Coolidge, and governor general of the Philippines. What other prominent political figures can you name with distinguished careers in collegiate and/or professional athletics? It may require research to find out. As a class, determine how many names you can find, their political accomplishments, and their athletic successes.

Cricketeer

If you ask U.S. citizens to name some legendary athletes, they may name Mantle or Aaron, Jordan or Johnson, or many others; it would be a rare individual who would name Grace. Yet William Gilbert (W. G.) Grace was perhaps the most phenomenal athlete of his time and arguably the most famous man of Victorian England. Due to his excellence, thousands of people flocked to the cricket fields to see the game, just as long as they could see Grace as well.

W. G. Grace was an amateur English cricketeer whose playing career lasted from 1865 to 1908. When he retired in 1908, he had earned nearly 55,000 runs and taken almost 3,000 wickets in first-class cricket. He was still the opening batsman for England when he was 50 years old.

Grace was born in Downend, Gloucestershire, England, on July 18, 1848. He always had a love for cricket, so it is no surprise that he spent a lifetime playing it, beginning at age 17 and playing until he was 60. Always an excellent player, Grace's two best seasons came in 1871 and 1876. In 1871 he totalled more than 2,700 runs in 39 innings, becoming the first player to score more than 2,000 in one season. In 1876 he scored 344 runs for Marylebone Cricket Club against Kent, 177 runs for Gloucestershire against Nottinghamshire, and 318 "not out" against Yorkshire, all in consecutive innings. Grace also captained the first English Test Match against Australia in 1880. It was a bittersweet day when this giant of the cricket field retired from the game he had dominated for four decades.

Part of the reason Grace's fame, as well as the popularity of cricket, spread was the fact that railroad travel made it possible for cricket teams to travel easily around the country, allowing many to see them play in person.

Cricket became highly respectable. It came to represent part of the code of honor and respectability cherished by English gentlemen. Not only was it manly, but it was "decent" as well.

W. G. Grace died in 1915 at the age of 67.

Suggested Activities

Cricket: Learn to play the game! Your local library is sure to have one of many books available on the basics of the sport. Learn them as part of your physical education exercises.

Statistics: Follow the play of some popular cricketeers today. Keep track of their statistics and use them for mathematical exercises.

46

The Tour de France

The most popular bicycle race in the world today, the Tour de France, had its start all the way back in 1903. Although the bicycle was widely used for exercise and leisure in France at the turn of the century and had been for 50 years, Henri Desgranges, a French cyclist, thought the sport needed something extra. He mapped a 2,400-kilometer (about 1,500 miles) route through France, ending along the Champs Élysées. Scores of cyclists turned out to compete, racing through the course's six stages.

Today, more than 200 cyclists gather and race through multiple stages along a course of about 3,200 kilometers (approximately 2,000 miles), over a period of 25 to 30 days. The route changes each year, although most of it remains within France. The course has also included stages through England, Germany, Belgium, Spain, and Switzerland.

The Tour de France is divided into many stages, and each stage usually takes place over one day. Stages often feature a specific cycling skill such as hill climbing or sprinting, and each stage is timed. The leader after each day's stage (cumulative with the previous days' times) wears the *maillot jaune* (yellow jersey). Observers can always tell the current lead cyclist by the jersey he wears. The winner at the end of the entire Tour receives the yellow jersey as a trophy of the race.

Individuals in the race do not compete alone. Every individual is part of a team. *Domestiques* help their team leader to win the race by acting as wind shields, by supplying the leader with food or drink along the way, or simply by encouraging the leader along the route. Coaches, doctors, cooks, and bicycle mechanics are also integral to each team. All prize moneys are usually divided by the leader amongst the team.

As one might imagine, the cost of riding in the Tour de France can be very expensive. The equipment, time, lodgings, and more cost a vast amount of money. For that reason, teams are sponsored by corporations which provide financial support. Such corporations also supply a team vehicle that follows behind its racers, ready with provisions and bicycle-repair equipment.

When the Tour de France began in 1903, it was enormously successful and popular. However, in the second year, foul play marred its image. Overeager fans put tacks on the road as well as roadblocks to get in the way of opposing cyclists. French officials quickly rallied and put together provisions to keep such interference out of the Tour.

The Tour, which has been run every year since 1903 with the exception of the World War I and II years, draws competitors and spectators from around the world. The last stage (and more) of the Tour de France is often televised.

The most frequent winners of the race are Europeans; however, cyclist Greg LeMond became the first American to win in 1986. He won again in 1989 and 1990. Other great winners include Miguel Indurain of Spain who dominated the nineties, and Jacques Anquetil (France), Bernard Hinault (France), and Eddy Merckx (Belgium), who have each won five Tours. Maurice Garin, a chimney sweep, was the first Tour winner; he had an overall time of 94.5 hours.

The Tour de France is longer and has more stages today than it did when it began, but the principle is the same. Riders compete to determine who is the fastest and best cyclist in the world.

Suggested Activity

Cycling: Learn about cycling safety, repair, and race performance. If possible, allow students to bring their bikes to school to learn through the hands-on approach.

Earthquake!

San Francisco was a booming and prosperous port town in 1906, but at 5:13 A.M. on April 18, all that changed. A massive earthquake struck the city and surrounding area. Fires broke out throughout the city due to severed electric lines, overturned lamps, and the explosions of gas mains. To make matters worse, the city's water mains were also damaged, retarding the firefighters' ability to fight the raging flames. For three days the flames spread, largely unchecked. Finally, firefighters began dynamiting blocks of buildings just to stop the fire from spreading. When the damage was assessed, 3,000 lives were lost, 250,000 people were homeless, and more than 28,000 buildings were destroyed. Damage to property was in excess of 500 million dollars.

A strong earthquake struck the city again in 1989; however, this time only 12 lives were lost. The difference was largely due to architectural and technological advances that have made newer buildings better able to withstand powerful earthquakes.

Suggested Activity

To learn more about some kinds of earthquakes, try the experiments below.

Materials: cardboard box, metal pan, uncooked beans or rice, deck of cards, dominoes, building blocks

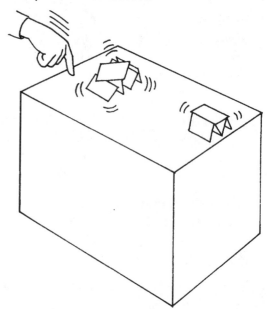

Procedure:

1. Begin with the cardboard box. Turn it upside down. Build two small houses of cards, one near the edge of the box and one further away.

2. Tap your fingers gently eight to ten times on the box in front of the closest house. Watch the movement of both houses. You should see that the house closest to the tapping receives the most damage, although the walls of both houses will shift position. The different effects are caused by waves of energy sent by the tapping (earthquake). The vibrating energy weakens as it travels.

3. Repeat the experiment, this time with two houses of dominoes. Watch the results.

4. Repeat it once more, this time with block houses. Again, watch the results. The three kinds of structures will show the ability different structures have to withstand earthquakes.

5. If desired, the three different housing materials can be built on different surfaces and the experiment repeated. This will show how the various surfaces alter the effects of a quake's energy waves. After the cardboard box, try an overturned metal pan. Next, invert the pan, and fill it with dry rice or beans, and then build the structures on them. What happens in each scenario?

Flight

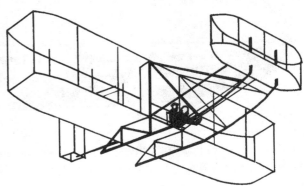

At the turn of the century, very few believed that flight was possible in a heavier-than-air machine. Two of the few who did believe were Wilbur and Orville Wright. Wilbur Wright was born in 1867 in Indiana, and Orville was born four years later in Ohio. As children the two were fascinated by mechanics and even earned small amounts of money by selling homemade mechanical toys. Both went to school, but neither received a high school diploma. When they grew up, Orville built a printing press and started a printing business, developing a weekly newspaper which Wilbur edited. Next, they tried their hands at renting and selling bicycles, and finally they began to manufacture the bikes themselves.

In 1896 the brothers read about the death of a glider pioneer named Otto Lilienthal, and his work sparked their interest. They started to read everything available on aeronautics and soon became as expert on the subject as any pioneer could be. The Wrights then contacted the National Weather Bureau to determine the best place to carry out their experiments with flight. The Bureau advised them to try a narrow strip of sandy land called Kill Devil Hill near Kittyhawk, North Carolina. In 1900 they tested a glider that could hold a person, and in 1901 they tried again with a larger glider. Neither glider could lift as they had hoped, although they did achieve some success in controlling balance.

The Wright brothers felt confident that flight was possible; therefore, they theorized that previous data concerning air pressure on curved surfaces must be inaccurate. They built their own wind tunnel and over 200 model wings in order to make their own pressure tables. Their tables became the first reliable ones ever made.

In 1902 they tried a third glider, using their new information. It vastly exceeded the success of both previous gliders, with some glides exceeding 600 feet (180 meters). This led the brothers to plan and build a power airplane. In 1903, at a cost just under one thousand dollars, the plane was completed. Its wings measured 40.5 feet (12 meters), and it weighed 750 pounds (340 kilograms) with a pilot. In September of 1903, they arrived in Kittyhawk, but a series of bad storms and technical problems delayed them. However, on December 17, 1903, they achieved flight.

Over the next few years, their experiments produced even longer and better flights. On October 5, 1905, their plane flew for 24.2 miles (38.9 kilometers) in just over 38 minutes. In 1908, they closed a contract with the United States Department of War for the first military airplane ever made.

The brothers went on to exhibit flight in France and the United States as well as to teach others to be pilots. Eventually, the inevitable happened: on September 17, 1908, Orville and his passenger, Lieutenant Thomas E. Selfridge, crashed due to a malfunction. Orville recovered, but Selfridge died. However, the work of the brothers continued until Wilbur died of typhoid fever in 1912. Orville carried on alone until his death in 1948. Today they are remembered as the fathers of modern flight.

Suggested Activity

Models: Construct model airplanes from paper, testing their aerodynamic qualities. Conduct experiments and use your data to build the best possible plane. An excellent resource is Teacher Created Materials #281, *Thematic Unit: Flight.*

Zeppelins

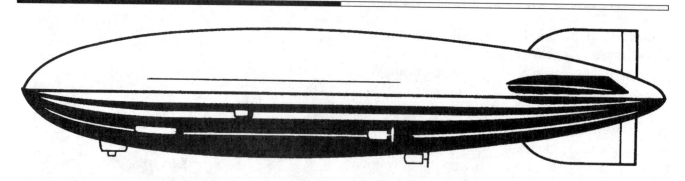

Airships, also called dirigibles, are lighter-than-air flying vehicles with engines to move them through the air and steering that allows them to be controlled. Hot air balloons and blimps were the primary method of human flight throughout the 1800s, but it was in the early 1900s that the best remembered type of airship, the Zeppelin, was developed and ruled supreme.

Henri Giffard, a French engineer, developed the first powered and manned airship in the mid-nineteenth century. It used a non-rigid, cigar-shaped gas bag with a three-horsepower (2.2-kilowatt) steam engine and a rudder supported below it in a gondola. In 1884 two French inventors named Charles Renard and Arthur Krebs completed the airship *La France* with a battery-powered electric motor (about 9-horsepower/7-kilowatt), rudder, and elevator. Brazilian inventor Alberto Santos-Dumont flew around the Eiffel Tower in an airship in 1901, earning him great popularity around the world.

In the midst of this, Count Ferdinand von Zeppelin was developing his own airship. His design featured a rigid frame which held individual gas cells. In 1900 he flew his first, called the *LZ-1*. It could reach a top speed of approximately 17 miles (27 kilometers) per hour. He followed this airship with the *LZ-2* in 1905 and the *LZ-3* in 1906. It was the *LZ-3* that the German army procured, and it became the first military Zeppelin. It was of supreme use to them in the next decade during World War I.

Another first for flight came in the first decade. In 1909 Count von Zeppelin developed the first commercial airline, DELAG. Commercial flights in Zeppelins remained popular for several years. However, their use came to an abrupt halt with the explosion of the *Hindenburg* in 1937. From that time on, the airplane has set the exclusive standard for commercial flight.

Suggested Activities

World War I: Research to determine the ways in which the Germans used Zeppelins during World War I. Compare their success with the airplanes developed in the United States.

Hindenburg: Find out why the *Hindenburg* exploded and what happened to its passengers.

David Schwarz: Schwarz is another important name in the development of airships. However, while his ideas were sound, his airship crashed. Determine what contributions he made to the development of airships.

Hot Air Balloons: If you live in an area where hot air balloons are commonly flown, take a field trip to explore them up close. Compare such balloons with the Zeppelin, making a chart that shows their similarities and differences.

Goodyear Blimps: Probably the most famous airships in use today are the Goodyear blimps. Find out how they operate and why they are used.

Pavlov's Dogs

For Ivan Petrovich Pavlov, dogs certainly were man's best friend.

Pavlov was a Russian physiologist who, in the early 1900s, experimented with dogs and other animals to prove that certain reflex responses can become conditioned responses to new, unrelated stimuli. The best known experiments conducted by Pavlov involved a dog, a bell, and meat. Pavlov knew that the dog's natural reflex at the smell of meat was to salivate. He began to ring a bell every time a dog was presented with meat. Eventually, Pavlov had only to ring the bell, and even though no meat was present, the dog began to salivate anyway. The animal's response had become conditioned, transferred to the new stimulus of the bell.

In 1904, Ivan Pavlov won the Nobel Prize for physiology and medicine. The award was granted for his research concerning digestion. He found that the vagus nerve controls the flow of the stomach's and pancreas' digestive juices.

Ivan Pavlov

Suggested Activities

Experiment: The students are probably already familiar with how their pets become excited at the sound of a can opener, believing it to be the animal's food. However, Pavlov showed something a little more: the animal's physiological response actually changed due to the stimulus of the bell. It was not merely that he became excited with the sound of the bell.

The best way to learn about Pavlov's work is clearly to conduct experiments such as his on your own. If space and time allow, conduct similar experiments with a mouse or other small animal that you can easily care for in your classroom. Do not be concerned for the animal's safety since such learned responses do the animal no harm whatsoever.

To begin, brainstorm and discuss with the class other ways in which they may have witnessed the same results that Pavlov got during his research. Also brainstorm for ways in which the class can conduct similar experiments. Remind them that the point is to transfer a physiological response from a natural stimuli to an artificial stimuli. Be sure to carefully follow and log your progress and results.

Scientific Research: Pavlov won the Nobel Prize for his research. If you do not wish to recreate experiments and research like Pavlov's, be sure to allow the students to conduct their own research on other scientific topics, carefully keeping records of all they hypothesize and do, as well as the results.

The Mad Scientists

Every now and then, the world meets an individual who, early in his career, may have been ridiculed or scorned for his "crazy" ideas—ideas that are later shown to be nothing less than genius. Two such men were Max Planck and Albert Einstein.

In 1900 a German theoretical physicist, Max K. E. L. Planck, proposed a law of radiation including a quantum theory; and the field of physics was completely revolutionized. Up until that time, scientists believed that energy flowed continuously. However, this belief did not explain the absorption and emission of energy by matter. Planck's theory did.

Quantum theory shows that objects can only absorb and emit energy in tiny packets called *quanta* (the plural of "quantum"). To measure the energy of each quantum, one must multiply the frequency of the radiant energy *(f)* by a universal constant *(h)*, known as Planck's constant. Therefore, energy *(E)* equals the constant multiplied by the frequency *(hf)*, or $E = hf$. This is demonstrated in the example of a red and blue flame. Less energy (heat) is emitted from a red flame than from a blue flame because the frequency of red light is less than that of blue; thus, the heat from a red flame is cooler than the heat from a blue flame.

In 1905 three papers by a young German physicist named Albert Einstein were published in a physics journal; one introduced the special theory of relativity, which has come to be the most well-known and significant theory in the history of physics. It states that matter and energy are equivalent; the formula $E = mc^2$ expresses this relationship. *E* represents energy, *m* is mass, and *c* (for "constant") is the speed of light (which, in a vacuum, never changes). The speed of light is extremely high (about 186,000 miles per second), so the formula states that even a small mass holds a great deal of energy. Also, the theory holds that the speed of light is unchanging regardless of the motion of its source or an observer. This was a completely new concept, one which shattered the rules of classical physics. In classical physics, if someone travelling in a car at 50 mph throws a baseball at 30 mph toward a wall, we just add the two velocities together to get the speed at which the ball strikes the wall: 80 mph (if we set aside the effects of wind-resistance and gravity); and we know that, for the person in the car, the ball appears to be travelling at only 30 mph. However, special relativity tells us that light acts in a completely different manner and is unaffected by the motion of its source. So if our car could travel at half the speed of light and we turned on its headlights to shine on a wall in front of it, instead of the light travelling at one-and-a-half times the speed of light when it hits the wall—as classical physics tells us it should—the light hits the wall at only the speed of light; and this is true for both an observer standing at the wall and the driver of the car. Even though the driver is moving very fast and the observer is standing still, both of them see the light as travelling at the same speed! In relativity theory, the speed of light is not relative at all!

The special theory of relativity has a counterpart which Einstein published 10 years later. This theory, the general theory of relativity, concerned the effects of gravity on motion and superseded the gravity theory of Sir Isaac Newton. Einstein's completed theory of relativity and his work on atoms meant a great deal to the world of science. It was his dream that atomic energy would help the world tremendously, and so he was greatly disturbed by the fact that his work helped lead to the development of the atomic bomb.

In 1918, Planck won a Nobel Prize for his work. Einstein won a Nobel Prize in 1921.

Suggested Activity

Relativity: To demonstrate the relative nature of motion for everyday objects, have the students consider the following: A train with glass walls passes through a train station at 50 mph. On the train a child is throwing a ball up and down. How would a passenger on the train describe the motion of the ball? How about someone standing on the platform at the station? Or a passenger on a train passing by at 50 mph in the opposite direction? (See page 96 for answers and explanations.)

New York Underground

Subways have been in existence since London opened its first underground passenger line in 1863. It was built to expedite travel in the heavily populated city. People could go from one part of the city to another in just minutes, whereas the time on foot or by horse-drawn carriage would take much longer, particularly as it involved combating the many others above ground trying to do the same.

Immigration in the nineteenth century added vastly to the population of New York by the turn of the century. New York officials felt the best solution to traffic problems was to build a subway of their own. First opened in 1904, New York's subway is now one of the most extensive and famous in the world. The first line, the Interborough Rapid Transit (IRT), operates in Manhattan and a large section of the Bronx, with branches in Brooklyn and Queens. The Independent Subway (IND) has lines in all boroughs except Staten Island. The Brooklyn-Manhattan Transit Company (BMT) has lines in Brooklyn, Manhattan, and Queens.

Today, New York's subway is enclosed. However, when the trains were first constructed, they were "open air." This means that there were no roofs but merely benches attached to a flat base that rolled along the tracks. Ladies in tall and feathered hats, a popular style of the time, certainly needed to take care in those fast moving cars.

The New York subway is primarily an "open-cut" subway. This is made by tearing out the streets and building the subway in big ditches. When two lines are going to cross, one roadbed is dug at a deeper level than the other. A cover is often placed above such open–cut subways; it is then called a "cut and cover." Open–cut subways such as New York's are usually rectangular in shape, as opposed to tube subways (bored through the earth without displacing the surface), which are usually circular or semicircular.

The original subways were run by steam locomotives. Since 1890, all have been run by electricity. New York's subway, of course, has always used electricity.

Suggested Activities

Mass Transit: Subways were formed in order to move many people in a short amount of time. Discuss the pros and cons of such a venture. How is it helpful to society? How is it harmful? Consider also the other forms of mass transit commonly in use today. Which are the most effective?

Effectiveness: Although subways have proved beneficial in many parts of the world, other places resist them for a variety of reasons, including safety and cost. Research to determine which major cities use them and why, as well as the major cities that do not.

Crime: Research and consider the crime rates on subways, and discuss what precautions and preventative steps can be taken in the future. Ask the class what they would do if their commission was to try to make subways crime free.

The Father of Psychoanalysis

Born on May 6, 1856, Sigmund Freud grew to be one of the greatest researchers and theorists in the field of psychology. The eldest of eight children (two older brothers from his father's first marriage were adults when Sigmund was born), Freud lived in poverty throughout his early years. A Jewish philanthropic society paid for his medical education, and Freud became quite skilled and effective, particularly in the field of histology, the study of the structure of tissues. Freud then became a neurologist, married, and had children—all the while investigating new theories and ideas. Eventually, his focus shifted from the physiological to the psychological, or from the brain to the mind. It is for this work that Freud is most greatly remembered.

Sigmund Freud

In 1900, Freud published the work for which he is most noted, *The Interpretation of Dreams*. This book deals with dreams, the mechanics behind them, and the unconscious mind through which they are formed. From this work developed Freud's Wednesday Psychological Group, which later became the Vienna Psycho-Analytical Society, a group of colleagues and students who met to study Freud's investigations. Then in 1904, Freud published his very popular *The Psychopathology of Everyday Life*. This book studied imperfect mental functions, such as forgetting and slips of the tongue. The theories Freud presented in this book are more widely accepted today than any theories presented in his other works.

Freud led a very happy personal life with his wife and six children, but his professional life was not always so. Often, he was ridiculed and dismissed, as many great pioneers are. However, he had a well developed sense of humor, and his philosophy was to continue to present new evidence no matter what. He never stopped to argue with his critics.

As time went on, other analysts grew to accept, expand upon, and alter the work of Freud, most notably Carl Jung. Freud continued his investigations throughout it all. When Naziism sprang up in his homeland, Freud began to focus on the nature and origin of Judaism. This was the work he pursued throughout the remainder of his life.

Today, the entire field of psychoanalysis is said to have its roots in the work of Sigmund Freud.

Suggested Activities

Dream Journal: Over a period of one week, keep a journal of your dreams. Most analysts today believe that only the individual doing the dreaming can know for certain what the dreams mean, since individuals have their own symbologies. After a week, look over your dreams and determine what you think they mean.

Research: There are many dream dictionaries on the market which suggest ideas for what symbols in dreams mean. At your discretion, provide some of those meanings to the students and allow them to discuss their merits.

Anna Freud: The daughter of Sigmund Freud, Anna Freud grew up to be a psychoanalyst. Research to find out more about the life and work of Anna Freud.

Beatrix Potter and Peter Rabbit

Beatrix Helen Potter was born on July 6, 1866, in London, England. She lived there with her wealthy parents throughout most of the year, but the family spent their holidays in the country. It was there that Potter developed a familiarity with and a love for wild animals. Although she had difficulties in her life that made her unhappy, the animals and her imagination always gave her joy.

At age 27, Potter became an author of children's literature in an unusual way. She sent illustrated stories to a sick child. The stories were collected and printed privately in 1900. They were called *The Tale of Peter Rabbit*. In the following year, a publisher's edition that included her now famous watercolor drawings was printed. The delightful book is still in print today and continues to sell very well.

Potter wrote other children's books over the next several years, including *Squirrel Nutkin, Mrs. Tittlemouse,* and *Mr. Jeremy Fisher.* Although the animals are given personalities and voices, their natures remain consistent with those of real animals. Therefore, although the books are fanciful, they are also realistic, just as are Potter's illustrations.

When she was nearly 50 years old, Potter married a lawyer named William Heelis. The two lived on a farm called Hill Top in Sawrey, Lancashire. There, Potter raised sheep and lived in the natural setting she loved. When she died in 1943, her farm was bequeathed to the National Trust. It remains open to the public.

─── Suggested Activity ───

Drawing: Beatrix Potter took care to make her illustrations both realistic and fanciful. Have the students attempt their own realistic drawings. If possible, let them view some real animals and draw them. You can also have them attempt to duplicate other realistic drawings or photographs. They can begin by drawing them in the boxes below.

rabbit	rabbit
squirrel	squirrel

Just So

Rudyard Kipling is one of the most popular and prolific authors the world has known. He was the first author of his native England to win the Nobel Prize for Literature (1907).

Kipling was born in India to British parents. His parents, like other English parents, sent him to school in England when he was five. He boarded there with foster parents for five years and then later attended a school for sons of army officers, also in England. The unhappy tale of his early years in England became the subject of one of his first stories (1888), and the friendships, pranks, and adolescent brutalities of English public schools became the subject of another.

In all, Kipling received an adequate education, but since the family could not afford to send him to college, he returned to India. He had been active in journalism while in school, so he pursued the career and became a newspaperman. The papers he worked for printed some of his stories and poems in addition to his articles.

Rudyard Kipling

Throughout the later years of the nineteenth century, Kipling published many books, including *The Jungle Book* and *Captains Courageous*. Arguably his finest novel came in 1900. It was called *Kim*, and his excellent knowledge of Indian culture and people helped to make it an engaging and rich novel. It is considered a classic of British fiction. The book was followed by another favorite, Kipling's *Just So Stories* which tell humorous stories of how some natural things came to be (such as how the elephant got its trunk). In all, Kipling wrote more than 300 short stories, numerous novels, and many poems. It was for his complete body of work that the Nobel committee honored him in 1907.

Kipling died in 1937 while writing his autobiography.

Suggested Activities

Tell Me Why: Kipling used his imagination to explain how things came to be in his *Just So Stories*. Have the students write stories of their own. Preface their writing with the reading of some of Kipling's work as well as myths from various cultures. Then let them write their own and share them with the class. They can choose their own topics, or you can provide them with the following ideas:

- why snow is white
- why the snake slithers
- how the Andes Mountains were formed

- how the eagle got its wings
- how the cheetah got its spots
- why the lion has a roar

- why the ant is strong
- why the monkey has a tail
- how the orange got its peel

Comparison: Read *The Jungle Book* by Kipling. Then watch the Disney cartoon version as well as the live action version. Compare the three and discuss their merits.

The Funny Papers

People around the world read the funny pages in their newspapers each day, and they cannot imagine their papers without them. But before 1907, there were no funny pages. There was not even a comic strip. That all changed with a man named Bud Fisher.

Bud Fisher had an idea; and with the help of the *San Francisco Chronicle*, he made it a reality. Cartoonists had been drawing individual cartoons for quite awhile, but Fisher wanted to print a strip that would appear in the paper each day. The *Chronicle* liked the idea. Fisher's strip was called *Mr. Mutt*. Later he changed the name, and it became one of the most enduring strips of all time: *Mutt and Jeff*.

Suggested Activity

See You in the Funny Papers: Comic strips all share the same basic format. The problem, or setup, is presented in the first one of several panels, with the solution and punchline coming in the last panel. Write a comic strip of your own. You will need to create a set of characters that can repeat in the strip each day. The strip will need to tell or show a joke or something humorous. Use the panels below. (Delete any lines you want, or change your number of panels.)

Picasso and Cubism

It is said by many that no artist of the 1900s was more significant to the world of art than Pablo Picasso. He certainly was the dominant artist of the time.

Picasso created art in many forms: paintings, sculptures, prints, drawings, and ceramics. He also developed the style of collage, incorporating things such as wallpaper and newsprint in the work of art. Yet, perhaps he is best known for a brand new style which he pioneered. The style is called *cubism*.

At the turn of the century, impressionism, pointillism, and symbolism were the three prominent styles of art. Picasso experimented with them, but always he was reaching for something new—a new way to express himself artistically. In 1907, he fully captured his new style with jagged and distorted images. The painting that did this is called *Les Demoiselles d'Avignon*. Inspired by primitive art and Picasso's interest in African and Iberian sculptures, the painting revolutionized the art world in the 1900s. It should be said that at the same time, an artist named George Braque was independently creating a similar style. It is Picasso, however, whose name is indelibly linked with cubism.

Cubism is an entirely new way of seeing nature and art. From the time of the Renaissance, artists had been painting in a way that incorporated atmospheric and linear perspective. In the nineteenth century, a group of artists experimented with perspective, creating a balance between the three-dimensional illusion created by the painting and the two-dimensional nature of the canvas itself. However, with all the experimentation, there was really no distortion of objects and the space around them.

In 1907, Picasso and Braque demonstrated that a figure could be distorted and transformed from the traditional planes. From there, it was an easy step to see that a painting could consist of an abstract arrangement of lines, shapes, and colors. Cubism, it seems, was the beginning of nonobjective art. Just as Albert Einstein, a contemporary in the world of science, was beginning to show, perspective is relative.

Suggested Activities

Cubist Art: Your local library should have a variety of art texts that include prints of major works of art. Look through them to find Picasso's *Guernica* and *Three Musicians*, as well as *Les Demoiselles d'Avignon*. Also look for work by Braque and later cubists such as Juan Gris and Willem de Kooning. Compare and discuss the styles. Ask the students how cubism is different from realistic paintings. Also ask their opinions of the style.

Artists: Allow the students to attempt cubist works of their own. Provide them with an object, such as a vase of flowers or bowl of fruit, and ask them to draw or paint it in Picasso's style. Have the class choose and discuss the most successful attempts.

An American in Paris

Mary Cassatt was born in America in 1844, but she spent most of her life in France. Much of her art belongs to the great French impressionist movement. In the early part of the twentieth century, she was a preeminent and respected artist.

Mary Cassatt

Cassatt always considered herself an American (she is quoted as saying, "I am an American, definitely and frankly American"), but she believed that Europe, and particularly France, was the place to be for an artist. At first, her father, a prominent Philadelphia banker, disapproved of her going. He suggested she attend the Academy of Fine Arts in Philadelphia instead. She did, from 1861–1865, but it never satisfied her. She decided to stay with family friends in France, and her father made no objection to a visit. But for Cassatt, it became a lifetime.

Mary Cassatt was privileged not only with a great talent but also with the means to follow the career of her choice, though that was greatly uncommon for women of her time. Cassatt was independently wealthy, so she was able early in life to do things that women normally did not do. She did, in fact, become an important artist and, though alone, she lived far away from her home and family. This was unusual for women of her era, who usually married and raised families. Certainly, Cassatt never had any financial struggles, and her place in society was always secure due to the prominence of her family, so she did not have issues of money and consequence to hinder her. Even so, her choices for the time were rare, and she had her share of struggle making her mark.

Cassatt studied in Italy before making her home in Paris. There she continued to explore impressionism, a style of painting that seeks to show the effects of light on objects. She became very good friends with the noteworthy French Impressionist Edgar Degas. Like Degas, she began to show the influence of Japanese woodcuts in her art from 1882 onward.

Cassatt is best known for her typical subject matter, mothers and their young children. These subjects were not posed but were shown performing everyday activities, such as in her famous work *The Bath*. The mood of much of her work is serene and quiet. She captures the moments in typical expressionistic style: bright, light colors and sketchy brushstrokes, cleverly depicting what the eye may capture in a glance.

A proponent of the Impressionist movement, Cassatt urged American collectors to purchase impressionistic art. She succeeded in her attempts and is generally noted as having had influence on the spread and popularity of the movement.

In 1904 Mary Cassatt was awarded the French Legion of Honor for her work.

Suggested Activities

Career Choices: While Cassatt was a single woman, painting with the impressionists, most women of the time married, raised children, and ran their homes. Cassatt's work was not traditional. Ask the students if they could choose their life's career and family circumstances today, what they would be. Have them either discuss or write about these hopes and dreams.

Artists: Ask the students to create a work of art in honor of both Mary Cassatt and their own families. Each student can draw, color, or paint a picture of himself or herself as a young child with a special person who took care of him or her, perhaps his or her mother, father, or grandparent.

The Songwriter

Irving Berlin is the stage name of one of America's most popular and beloved songwriters. Born Isidore Baline in Russia in 1888, Berlin and his family moved to the United States in 1893. His father was a cantor who died in 1896, leaving the family financially destitute. Berlin went to work, selling newspapers and singing on the streets. He received no formal musical training and could not read or write music; however, while working as a singing waiter, he began to compose music and lyrics. In 1907, his first work, lyrics for the song "Marie from Sunny Italy," was published.

By 1909, Berlin had published over 20 songs. In 1910, he performed his own material in a vaudeville act. The following year, he published "Alexander's Ragtime Band," establishing his claim to national recognition. Continuing to publish his music, Berlin also wrote for the popular *Ziegfeld Follies* (page 62). In 1919, at age 31, he began his own music-publishing company. He followed this two years later with a partnership in the Music Box Theater of New York City, where he staged his musical reviews.

Over the course of his career, Irving Berlin published more than 1,500 songs. His works include lyrics and/or music for such shows as *Watch Your Step, The Century Girl, Annie Get Your Gun, Miss Liberty, Call Me Madam,* and *Mr. President,* and such movies as *Top Hat, On the Avenue, Blue Skies,* and *Easter Parade.* Among his most memorable songs are "There's No Business Like Show Business," "God Bless America," "Easter Parade," "White Christmas," "Everybody's Doin' It," and the aforementioned "Alexander's Ragtime Band."

Having received no musical training, Berlin chose his own methods of composition. He played on an upright piano, and he primarily used the black keys. He fitted the keys with a special lever which allowed for automatic transposition of the keyboard. His special piano now stands in the Smithsonian Institution, donated by Berlin in 1973.

In 1968, Berlin was awarded a special Grammy for Lifetime Achievement. Certainly his musical achievements were extensive and merited him the award. Berlin died in 1989 at the age of 101 after a long, prosperous, and prolific career. He is known today as an American musical legend.

Suggested Activities

Listen: Bring recordings of Irving Berlin's music into the classroom, and allow the students to listen to his musical compositions and lyrics. Discuss the commonalties among the songs and Berlin's typical style.

Composition: Challenge students to write lyrics and/or music for an original song. They will discover the difficulty of composing over 1,500 songs as they attempt to write just one!

Ragtime: Ragtime music reached its peak during the first decade of the twentieth century. Study the ragtime sound, listening to "Alexander's Ragtime Band" and other ragtime favorites such as Scott Joplin's "Maple Leaf Rag" (1899).

Theater: If a Berlin show is playing in your area, why not plan a field trip to see it as a class? You might also show a popular film for which he composed music such as *Easter Parade* or *Top Hat.*

Piano: Provide a lesson on playing the piano. Allow students to learn some keyboard rudiments. Alternatively, allow them to compose without any instruction, just as Berlin did.

Writing Music: Provide a lesson on musical notation, allowing students to learn the special language of music.

Greatest Tenor of the Century

Enrico Caruso, the great Italian tenor, was born in Naples, Italy, in 1873. He made his singing debut at the age of 21, and he immediately became successful. His Italian performances were followed quickly with engagements throughout Europe, and in 1903, he made his debut in America, performing at the Metropolitan Opera House in New York City. His performance in Giuseppe Verdi's *Rigoletto* became one of his most famous roles.

A tenor is the highest natural adult male singing voice. It carries the approximate range of two octaves, usually beginning at C below middle C.

Caruso sang primarily Italian operas. Some roles he created, while others he made famous. Perhaps his most well-known role is that of Canio in Ruggero Leoncavallo's *Pagliacci*.

Early in his career, Caruso exhibited some difficulty in maintaining voice control. This is attributed primarily to the inconsistent training he received. However, in time he gained a control that gave his natural tenor voice the additional timbre of a baritone, allowing him a broad range and a vocal quality that captivated his listeners.

Caruso became the biggest attraction at the Metropolitan Opera House, continuously bringing in packed houses and rave reviews. The power, beauty, and unique qualities of his voice made him an international star. When music began to be recorded on phonograph records, Caruso's voice was among the first to be replicated. Through the phonograph, Caruso's fame spread even more, and he became one of the most well–known men in the world.

Caruso's singing can still be heard through technological advancements that allow the old recordings to be preserved and reproduced. It is through this technology that people of the present and future can and will enjoy the rich tenor that made Caruso famous.

Caruso's final performance was on Christmas Eve, 1920. He died the following year. More than 60 years later, the National Academy of Recording Arts and Sciences honored Enrico Caruso with a Lifetime Achievement Grammy Award.

During his lifetime, Caruso was considered to be the greatest living tenor. Many critics today consider him the greatest tenor of all time.

Suggested Activities

Listen: Find a recording of Caruso and allow the students to listen. Discuss the power and beauty of his voice. Allow the students to discuss their probable unfamiliarity with opera and how it may strike them as funny at first. (In discussion, they should realize that its lack of familiarity in both style and language is what strikes their funnybones.)

My Voice: If there is a trained teacher of music in your school, ask him or her to come to the classroom to classify the students' voices. While Caruso was a tenor, your classroom should be filled with sopranos, contraltos, altos, basses, other tenors, and perhaps even a baritone. Play recordings of singers in these various ranges (for example, Joan Baez is an excellent example of a pure soprano), and allow students to compare what they hear. They may begin to discern the differences in pitch and range. Discuss why the human voice is considered an instrument.

Italian: Most of Caruso's singing was in Italian. As a class, learn some basic Italian words and phrases. Try to translate a lyric or two from Caruso's catalog of musical recordings.

Ziegfeld Follies

The year was 1907, and a Chicago-born theater producer developed one of the most enduring pieces of musical theater history. His name was Florenz Ziegfeld, and the show was the *Ziegfeld Follies*.

Ziegfeld was the son of the founder of the Chicago Musical College, so music surrounded him from the time of his birth. He met his wife in 1896 while producing a play, *A Parlor Match*, in which she was featured. The producer later developed several shows that featured his wife, Anna Held. These shows included songs, fine settings, and fancy costumes. They became the forerunner for the soon-to-be *Ziegfeld Follies*.

The *Follies* ran annually from 1907 through 1927, and Ziegfeld billed them "An American Institution," which indeed they became. They featured a chorus of beautiful women, elaborately costumed and in lavish and imaginative settings. The shows were always extravagant and lush, beautiful to behold. Ziegfeld withheld nothing in his productions, spending money freely. In fact, it is said that he was known to discard a set on which he had spent a great deal of money after it had been used in only one performance.

The shows were a treat for the ears as well as the eyes, for Ziegfeld hired such luminary composers as Irving Berlin and Jerome Kern to provide songs. He also hired a number of talented entertainers who became stars such as W. C. Fields, Will Rogers, Fanny Brice, Eddie Cantor, Paulette Goddard, Marion Davies, and Irene Dunne.

The Ziegfeld Follies began with an elaborate production that celebrated the Gibson Girl (page 66). The producer was always interested in bringing forward lovely women and glorifying (and capitalizing on) their beauty. Ziegfeld often used the slogan "Glorifying the American Girl." The Ziegfeld girls were slender and graceful, and they became models for feminine beauty.

There are a number of Hollywood movies that capture the spirit of *The Follies*, and some like *Funny Girl* (the story of Fanny Brice) tell actual accounts of the Follies and the people who performed in them. (Use your discretion in viewing *Funny Girl,* or excerpted scenes from it, as a class.)

Ziegfeld went on to produce other musicals such as *Rio Rita* and *Show Boat*. His marriage ended in divorce, but he married again in 1914 to the actress Billie Burke, best known as Glinda in *The Wizard of Oz*. He died in 1932.

Suggested Activities

History: Trace the history of musical theater in the United States and how *Ziegfeld Follies* has influenced later productions. Also learn about the lives and careers of famous *Follies* performers.

Performance: As a class, produce and stage a one-song musical production in the style of the *Ziegfeld Follies*. Design and make elaborate sets and costumes. Include both boys and girls in a dance production. View portions of some old Hollywood films to help give you ideas. The film *Easter Parade* includes a good sequence, and it is acceptable for all age groups.

Mother's Day

At the urging of Anna Jarvis of Grafton, West Virginia, Mother's Day was first celebrated on a large scale on May 10, 1908. Here is its history.

A day called Mothering Sunday originated in England many years ago. It took place in the middle of the Lenten (pre-Easter) season each year. Julia Ward Howe, the author of "The Battle Hymn of the Republic" and a suffragette, first suggested a Mother's Day in the United States in 1872. She thought the day should be dedicated to the observance of peace. For several years, she held annual observances of the day in Boston, but it did not gain national support. In 1887 a Kentucky teacher named Mary Towles Sasseen began annual Mother's Day celebrations, and in 1904, Frank E. Hering of Indiana did the same. But it was not until three years later that the interest was ignited in Anna Jarvis, and she began a campaign for the

Anna Jarvis

national observance of the holiday. She selected the second Sunday in May for the celebration. In May of 1908, churches in Grafton and Philadelphia began the tradition. A Grafton church devoted its service to the memory of Jarvis's mother, Anna Reeves Jarvis.

The Methodist Episcopalian Church to which Anna Jarvis belonged designated her as the founder of Mother's Day at a conference in 1912, and the conference also adopted her chosen date of the second Sunday in May for the observance. In May of 1914, President Woodrow Wilson signed a resolution recommending that the government recognize and observe Mother's Day, and in 1915 it was declared a national holiday.

Anna Jarvis began one more Mother's Day tradition. On the first Mother's Day, she wore a carnation in memory of her mother. Traditionally, people wear colored carnations if their mothers are living and white if they are not.

Suggested Activities

Mothers: Have the students write poems, make cards, or create other pieces of art to honor their mothers. Also discuss what it is that makes a good mother. Let the students share all their views.

Children: Some students wonder why there is a Mother's Day and a Father's Day but no Children's Day (although some cultures, such as the Japanese, do have such a day). Ask the students to discuss why they think this is. Also have them plan a Children's Day celebration or suggest some possible Children's Day traditions.

Holidays: Research to determine the origin of several national holidays. Have the students brainstorm for additional holidays they feel would be worthwhile.

Ford and the Tin Lizzie

The nineteenth century went out in a horse-drawn carriage; the twentieth century came in on motorized wheels. This was due in large part to world-renowned automotive tycoon Henry Ford.

Henry Ford was born in 1863 on a farm in what later became Dearborn, Michigan. In his early years, he was a machinist and an engineer with a growing interest in a new invention called the automobile. In 1893, he built his first successful gasoline engine, and by 1896, he had built his first automobile. Finally, in 1903, he began the Ford Motor Company.

In the first years of the century, automobiles were made one at a time with no standard parts. This process made them very expensive. Henry Ford wanted to bring cars to the masses. He decided that "the way to make automobiles is to make them all alike." So he designed a simple and reliable car that many people could afford: the Model T. They were all even the same color—black—and the car's slogan was "Any color you like as long as it's black."

The Model T, or Tin Lizzie as it affectionately came to be known, made its debut in 1908. The following year, Ford turned over his entire business to the production of Model Ts.

When Model Ts debuted, they cost $825, a reasonable price compared to other automobiles of the time but too high for the average citizen. Ford and his team of executive officers developed a plan to lower the cost of production. They determined that if employees in their factories worked on an assembly line, each employee responsible for the same task on each car, they could reduce the time it took to build one car from 12.5 hours to 1.5 hours, multiplying production considerably. This was an incredible savings. Ford passed on the savings to his customers and the increased profits to his employees. The cost of the Model T dropped to $550, $440, $345, and finally, $290 by 1924. This was a price that the average family could afford. Henry Ford also lowered his employees' work day from nine to eight hours and raised their pay to five dollars a day, about double that of workers in other plants. His employees also received part of the company's profits in Ford's profit-sharing plan.

For 20 years, the Model T outsold all other cars. In 1927, the last Model T, number 15,007,003, rolled off the line. The next several decades saw the rise of the General Motors Company, but Ford came back strong in the fifties and sixties under the leadership of Henry Ford's grandson.

In his later years, Henry Ford ran for public office and became involved in several charitable and peace-keeping ventures. Beside the incredible legacy of the Ford Motor Company, he left behind him the restored historical buildings of Greenfield Village and the Henry Ford Museum, which includes exhibits in science, industry, and art. Both sites are in Dearborn.

Suggested Activity

Assembly Lines: Choose a project that requires several steps, perhaps an arts and crafts project that involves tracing, coloring, cutting, and gluing. Have each student complete the project. Keep track of the time it takes each one. Then, divide the students into teams, each team having as many members as there are steps in the project. Have them complete the project in assembly line fashion (doing it several times for familiarity), timing them as they go. Compare the time for individual completion as opposed to teamwork. Also compare quality.

Wireless

Guglielmo is a rather unusual name, but Marconi certainly is not when it comes to the world of radio. Guglielmo Marconi was an Italian inventor who, in 1895, sent the first radio signals through the air. By 1901, he was able to send those signals all the way across the Atlantic Ocean.

Marconi was born in 1874. He was greatly interested in sound waves, and by the time he was 21 years of age, he had sent radio signals through the air instead of through the electric wires used in the telegraph system. The inventor used electromagnetic (radio) waves to send the signals, and his system of radio became known as wireless telegraphy.

A great day came in 1901. After effort, trial, and error, Marconi succeeded in sending waves across the

Guglielmo Marconi

Atlantic from Cornwall, England, to Newfoundland, Canada, a distance of more than 2,000 miles (3,300 kilometers). Though faint, the sound Marconi received was audible. This led the way for huge advancements, particularly concerning ships which used his technology to send distress signals when they were sinking or in trouble. Such radio communications also led to the capture and arrest of Dr. Crippen, a murderer, who was escaping aboard a cruise liner. He was the first murderer to be caught via radio while in flight.

Marconi sent his messages in Morse code. In 1906, American physicist Reginald Aubrey Fessenden made the first wireless broadcast of speech and music, paving the way for radio as we know it. Later in the same year, Fessenden pioneered two-way transatlantic wireless telegraphy.

Suggested Activities

Research: Research to learn more about the history of radio. If available, bring in samples of radios from previous decades. Learn about the type of transmissions they used and what technological advancements make today's radios so clear and strong.

Listen: As a class, listen to a limited number of radio minutes on each of various stations. (Use your own discretion.) Have the students write comparisons of the broadcasts, particularly comparing their cultural, social, and informative value.

Brainstorm: Throughout the century, the radio has had many uses. Brainstorm and research as many as the class can name.

Charles Gibson and His Girls

The pinnacle of feminine style at the turn of the century was the creation of Charles Dana Gibson, and she was called the Gibson Girl. A Gibson Girl is poised, athletic, attractive, and intelligent, and she represents the best of society. Many women of the early twentieth century strove to imitate the Gibson Girl; others merely idolized her.

Charles Gibson

Gibson himself was an illustrator, born in Roxbury, Massachusetts, who achieved quite an extensive fame through his creation. It is interesting to note that in his early years, this famed illustrator never cared to draw. Scissors were his tool of choice. He would cut silhouettes freehand of every subject—from farm animals, to the circus, to the people he knew. Amazingly, he did most of the cutting purely from memory, making entire scenes in one sheet of paper. As a child, Gibson is recorded as having told his mother, "They read such a nice story in the class today. See, I will make you a picture of it."

Charles Gibson is also noteworthy for his hand in the evolution of the bathing suit for women. A popular song of the time, which originated in the *Ziegfeld Follies*, has the beautiful Gibson Girl singing out,

> *So one day we rose*
>
> *In revolt of long clothes,*
>
> *And presented this tearful petition:*
>
> *Mister Gibson, Mister Gibson!*
>
> *Why can't we take a swim?*
>
> *Gibson complied.*

━━━ Suggested Activity ━━━

Silhouettes: You can cut your own silhouette images, even without the memory and skilled hand of Charles Dana Gibson.

Materials—magazines and newspapers, scissors, black paper, brightly colored or white paper, glue stick

Directions—Look through the magazines and newspapers to find an image with a striking silhouette (outline) that appeals to you. Cut around the image. Glue it to the black paper, being sure that the entire surface is fastened down. Cut around the outline of the image. Turn it over. Glue the picture side to a circle or square of the colored or white paper. You now have a silhouette image.

Dressing for the New Century

The look of the new century was full, colorful, and even flamboyant. Women's clothing was influenced by the Edwardian fashions of the last century, using lace and bows with elaborate hats to accent the outfits. Also popular was the Gibson Girl look and French *couture* from such designers as Paul Poiret. Women's hemlines varied from floor length to just above the ankles, while girls' dresses were knee length. Waists were slightly dropped, blouses were gathered in the front, and shoes were pointed and often high-topped. The permanent wave for hair was introduced in 1909. Men customarily wore suits with spats and high-topped shoes. Suit styles varied little over the decade. Men usually wore hats, although their hats were not as fanciful as women's. Boys' clothes were like men's, but boys wore short pants or knickers.

Typical outfits from the era are shown here and on the following page. Use them to study or to color.

Suggested Activity

Challenge: Design other clothing in typical 1900s styles.

Dressing for the New Century *(cont.)*

Elsewhere

This chronology gives a few of the important events around the globe during the first decade of the 1900s. Have students further research any people and events that interest them.

1900

- Boer War is in its third year.
- Boxer Rebellion unsettles China.
- Italian monarch is murdered.
- Max Planck formulates the quantum theory.

1901

- Australia becomes a commonwealth and joins the British Empire.
- Queen Victoria of England dies.
- Marconi transmits a telegraphic message across the Atlantic.

1902

- Mount Pelée erupts in the Caribbean.
- Aswan Dam of Egypt is opened.
- Triple Alliance is renewed among Germany, Italy, and Austria-Hungary.

1903

- Serbian monarchs are assassinated.
- Britain and France strike the Entente Cordiale.
- Mensheviks and Bolsheviks of Russia are formed.

1904

- Japan and Russia go to war.
- Captain Scott explores the Antarctic.
- Revolution erupts in German Southwest Africa.

1905

- Revolution starts in Russia.
- Norway's parliament separates from Sweden. Prince Charles of Denmark is made king.
- Sinn Fein party is founded in Ireland.

1906

- Rebellion breaks out in Tanganyika.
- Mount Vesuvius in Italy erupts.
- Night-shift work for women is internationally outlawed.

1907

- Congo Free State is purchased by the Belgian government.
- Mohandas Gandhi demonstrates peaceful resistance in South Africa.
- New Zealand becomes a British dominion.

1908

- A crisis exists in the Balkans, and there is the threat of war in Europe.
- Britain and Germany escalate their arms race.
- Ancient civilization of Knossos is discovered by Sir Arthur Evans.

1909

- Rioting takes place in Spain.
- Sultan of Turkey is deposed.
- North Pole is reached by Peary and Henson.

Olympic Highlights

Any study of the Olympic games of the early 20th century should start with a look at the first modern Olympics of 1896. Significant occurrences from 1896–1908 are listed below.

1896

- First modern Olympic games are held in Athens, Greece. They are created in the "hope for world peace" by French thinker and educator Pierre de Coubertin.
- Coubertin becomes the International Olympic Committee president (1896–1925).
- There are approximately 300 athletes from 15 countries competing in 43 events in 9 sports.
- The events at this Olympics are cycling, fencing, gymnastics, target shooting, swimming, tennis, track and field, weightlifting, and wrestling. Officials hoped to combine ancient Greek sports (such as discus throwing) with modern sports (such as cycling).
- No women compete.
- There are no winter games or events. The Winter Olympics will not begin until 1924.
- There is no Olympic flag or torch. They are added in 1920 and 1936, respectively.
- World response and reaction to the Olympics is limited, and press coverage is sparse.

1900

- The second modern Olympic games are held in Paris, France, during a World Exhibition.
- Female golfers and tennis players compete. No more sports for women are added this decade.
- The performances at this Olympics are not stellar. For example, the winner of the 100-meter race, American Thomas Burke, finishes in twelve seconds, one full second longer than the world record.
- Americans dominate this Olympics.
- The highlight of these Olympic games is the marathon victory by Greek athlete Spyridon Louis in the first ever marathon of the modern Olympics.
- These Olympics are held in conjunction with a World Exhibition. The fair overshadows them.

1904

- The first American Olympics are held in St. Louis, also at a World's Fair. The fair dominates.
- Performances at this Olympics are also lackluster.

1906

- Greece hosts the Intercalated Games. They are not recognized by the International Olympic Committee; however, most record books include these games.

1908

- The fourth modern Olympics are held in London, England.
- The first Asian member is elected to the International Olympic Committee.
- American and British competition is fierce. When an Italian runner, Dorando Pietri, collapses near the end of the marathon, British officials carry him across the finish line, keeping the American Johnny Hayes from winning. After protests, Hayes is declared the winner.
- Figure skating is added to the summer games. It is the first winter sport to be included.

Suggested Activities

Events: In small groups, make a list of the events conducted at the 1900, 1904, or 1908 Olympic games. Describe each event.

Compare: Compare an event from a 1900, 1904, or 1908 Olympics to that event today. How has it changed? How is it the same?

Women: Women had very small roles in the Olympics of the nineteen hundreds. Find out when and in which events they began to become more active.

Passages

Births

1900
- Thomas Wolfe, American writer
- Kurt Weill, German composer
- Aaron Copeland, American composer

1901
- Walt Disney, film producer and theme park creator
- Enrico Fermi, Nobel Prize-winning physicist

1902
- William Walton, English composer
- John Steinbeck, American novelist

1903
- Evelyn Waugh, English novelist

1904
- Graham Greene, English novelist
- Marlene Dietrich, German-born actress
- Salvador Dali, Spanish painter
- George M. Balanchine, Russian–born choreographer

1905
- C. P. Snow, English writer

1906
- Samuel Beckett, Irish author
- Greta Garbo, Swedish-born actress

1907
- W. H. Auden, English poet

1908
- Ian Fleming, English author, creator of the James Bond character

1909
- Robert Helpmann, British-Australian ballet dancer and choreographer

Deaths

1900
- Oscar Wilde, Irish poet, dramatist, and novelist
- Friedrich Nietzsche, German philosopher
- Stephen Crane, American author

1901
- Queen Victoria, British monarch
- Henri Toulouse-Lautrec, French artist
- Giuseppe Verdi, Italian composer

1902
- Cecil Rhodes, British financier and originator of the Rhodes scholarship
- Elizabeth Cady Stanton, American suffragette
- Samuel Butler, English author
- Emile Zola, French writer and critic

1903
- King Alexander I and Queen Draga of Serbia
- Pope Leo XIII
- Herbert Spencer, English philosopher
- James Whistler, American painter
- Paul Gauguin, French painter

1904
- Anton Chekhov, Russian playwright and short story writer

1905
- Jules Verne, French author

1906
- P. L. Dunbar, African–American poet
- Henrik Ibsen, Norwegian dramatist
- Paul Cézanne, French artist
- Pierre Curie, Nobel Prize-winning French physicist

1907
- Oscar II, King of Sweden
- Shah of Persia

1908
- King Carlos I, Portuguese monarch
- T'zu-hsi, Chinese Empress
- Grover Cleveland, former United States president

1909
- Frederick Remington, American artist
- King Leopold II of the Belgians

Boer War

The new century dawned under the cloud of war. Through the latter portion of the nineteenth century, the British had been enlarging their empire, including regions of Africa. However, the Boers (now Afrikaners), primarily farmers of Dutch heritage living in the northern South African regions of the Orange Free State and the South African Republic (later Transvaal), did not want to be under British rule. They also objected to the *Uitlanders* (foreigners), who were mainly British subjects. The South African Republic had been annexed by Britain in 1877. In 1880 and 1881, the Boers fought for and won independence. This battle is sometimes referred to as the First Boer War.

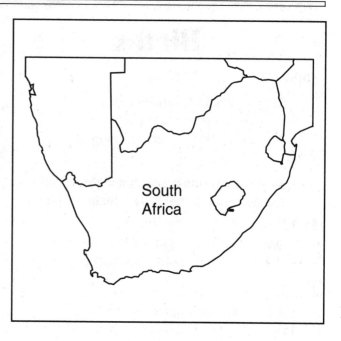

South Africa

The turmoil continued a few years later. In 1886, gold was discovered in the Witwatersrand field, and Uitlanders rushed to garner some of the wealth. Although the Boers fought politically to keep them out, the Uitlanders continued to battle against them. Peaceful attempts to settle failed, and so the Orange Free State and the South African Republic declared war on Britain in 1899. Interestingly, many Europeans, including some British, opposed British policy in South Africa prior to and during the war.

The beginning of the war was successful for the Boers, and they won many battles; however, war heroes Lord Roberts and Lord Kitchener arrived with a number of British troops in 1900 and turned the tide of the war. The Boer Army, under the leadership of General Botha, finally had to surrender in September of 1900. Guerrillas, however, continued to fight, but they, too, surrendered in May of 1902. The Orange Free State and the South African Republic became British colonies, and the Boers swore allegiance to King Edward VII.

The British agreed not to retaliate against or punish the Boers for their actions during the war. The Treaty of Vereeniging was signed on May 31, 1902.

Suggested Activities

Geography: Locate the pertinent regions (including Holland) on a current world map. Use atlases and other reference books to document the political changes in the regions from the start of the century to its close.

War Heroes: Lord Roberts, Lord Kitchener, and General Louis Botha were all heroes of the Boer War. Learn more about them and discuss their achievements. Hold a class discussion on the question: Who was the greatest soldier?

Empire: Determine all the colonies and holdings of the British Empire at the turn of the century. Discuss the justifications (or lack thereof) for the British nation to hold and govern so many countries around the world.

The Congo

In the course of the nineteenth century, European and American explorers discovered the economical value of trade and exploitation of the Congo (now Zaire). However, such perpetual exploitation caused widespread civil unrest. Moreover, international disputes concerning territorial rights led to the creation of the Berlin Conference of 1884, which opened the Congo Free State to trade with all nations, and the abolition of the slave trade. This new state was placed under the direct sovereignty of King Leopold I of Belgium in July 1885.

Congo (currently Zaire)

In 1904, continued unrest and protest, as well as increasing knowledge of horrific conditions for people in the Congo Free State, led to Leopold's forced establishment of a commission of inquiry. The commission discovered extensive slave labor and a variety of other abuses. Belgium's parliament then voted to annex the state and to make it a colony instead. It became the Belgian Congo.

Industry within the Belgian Congo grew considerably over the years, and a variety of reforms took place in order to move the state toward independence. In 1957, Africans in the area were able to vote for the first time. Out of this election, the independent Republic of the Congo was declared on June 30, 1960. However, internal disputes began almost immediately. Belgian and United Nations forces were placed at odds within the nation. Then the Union of Soviet Socialist Republics and the United States of America added their input and assistance to the various sides. Disputes and conflict continued throughout the sixties, with the government often changing hands.

In 1971, the nation's name was changed to Zaire. The new president attempted a complete overhaul of the government and culture, urging Africanization wherever possible. Foreign interests were taken over by Zaire, and people were urged to dismiss their non-African names.

In the eighties and nineties, economic concerns became the chief problem of Zaire, as well as the mass immigration of Rwandan refugees. Ethnic war in Rwanda forced more than one million citizens to flock along the Zaire border. Also in the nineties, the country made several attempts to become a democracy. This process is still undergoing change.

Although the country has changed hands and governments over the course of the century, it seems as much in a state of unrest today as it did when the century opened. Once the Congo, now Zaire, it remains in a state of flux.

Suggested Activities

Moments in Time: Break into small groups and choose a different period of time within the twentieth century. Study the political history of Zaire during this time.

Slavery: Learn about the slave trade and its roots in the Congo as well as its effect on the area.

Then and Now: Compare the Congo of 1900 to Zaire of the present day. How are they alike and different?

Peary, Henson, and the North Pole

At the start of the twentieth century, the Arctic Circle was largely uncharted, and no known person had travelled to the icy North Pole. Robert Edwin Peary set out to change all that.

In the late 1800s, Peary explored the interior and north of Greenland, proving that Greenland was an island and also making a variety of scientific discoveries about polar areas. These ventures ignited his interest in the Arctic region.

In 1898, Peary attempted to reach the North Pole. He set out in a ship called the *Windward*, and though he was gone for four years, he never reached the Pole. Instead, he reached a latitude of 84° 17' 27", which is approximately 390 miles (630 kilometers) south of the North Pole. Although this was a record (no one had ever traveled so far north), he had not reached his goal.

A few years later, in 1905, Peary tried once more, this time on the *Roosevelt*. This special ship was designed to sail among floes, which are masses of moving ice. The ship was able to travel as far north as Ellesmere Island. Peary and his crew continued northward on sledges over the icy Arctic Ocean. He and his group reached latitude 87° 6', a distance 200 miles (320 kilometers) south of the Pole. Again, he had set a record but missed his goal.

Throughout his expeditions, Peary traveled with another explorer named Matthew Alexander Henson. Henson was part of Peary's team for more than twenty years, acting as chief assistant and dog driver, a vital job in ice- and snow-covered areas. Henson was also noteworthy as an African American in an occupation usually reserved for white Americans. He told of his experiences in his 1912 book, *A Black Explorer at the North Pole.*

A third attempt to reach the North Pole began in 1908, and Peary and his party (a group consisting of four Eskimos and Henson) traveled on sledges from Ellesmere Island once more. They were able to reach latitude 89° 57', 3 miles (5 kilometers) from the Pole. The group became too tired to continue. They slept for a few hours, and then Peary and two Eskimos (Henson and the other two Eskimos stayed behind) decided to push onward. They crisscrossed the area to be sure they actually stepped foot on the location of the pole. The date was April 6, 1909, and Peary had finally reached the North Pole.

While at the Pole, Peary took soundings which proved the Arctic at the Pole was not shallow, as had been previously believed. He also took photographs. When Peary and his crew returned, others were skeptical. One man, Frederick A. Cook, claimed to have already reached the Pole. However, Cook's claims proved false, and the U.S. Congress gave credit to Peary. In 1988, the *National Geographic*, which had helped to support Peary's expedition, had Peary's claims investigated by a British explorer named Wally Herbert. Herbert's investigation raised questions about the validity of Peary's expedition. However, in 1989 a new study was made, concluding that Peary's camp was no further than 5 miles (8 kilometers) from the Pole, and that Peary did indeed reach it. Photographs showing the sun's position at the time as well as Peary's ocean soundings helped to support his claim.

Peary was finally vindicated. He died in 1920. Henson lived until 1955.

——— Suggested Activity ———

Geography: Draw maps of the Arctic area, including latitude lines that show the location of the North Pole.

74

Pogroms and the Pale of Settlement

When the new century began, anti-Jewish sentiment was well in place. As early as 1871, Russian soldiers, called *Cossacks*, carried out mob attacks in which Jewish homes and businesses were burned and people killed. These attacks were called *pogroms*. It is said that they lasted until 1906, although certainly anti-Jewish behavior did not end with them. The horrors of the coming Holocaust would prove that.

Violence against and oppression of Jews goes back in history for thousands of years. In Europe in the eighteenth century, Jews were not allowed to live in Russia, and, in fact, a Pale of Settlement was drawn, restricting Jews from many other countries as well. The Pale continued to remain in place for many years (laws finally removed it in 1917), and there were even towns within the Pale that did not allow Jews to reside or

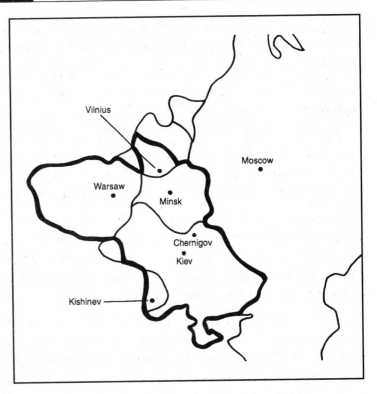

work there. Often, they were allowed to hold only certain jobs in the places where they did reside. Jews frequently lived in a state of poverty. Violence against them was commonplace. Despite the violence against them, Jewish males were often forced to defend Russia in the service of the Russian army for 25 years.

In June of 1906, peasant mobs attacked a Jewish settlement, killing hundreds. The peasants claimed to the police that the Jews had fired on a religious service, killing several children and a priest. The police, without any true investigation, took the side of the peasants. They distributed fliers throughout Russia, declaring that all Jews should be destroyed.

Although there was talk in the Russian legislature of attempting to stop violence against Jews, little was done. Persecution continued almost unchecked. This was perhaps the greatest catalyst for the mass migration of Jews to America in the nineteenth and early twentieth centuries.

Suggested Activities

History: Read about and discuss the Holocaust. Use your discretion. There are countless excellent resources available, but some may be too disturbing for your students' age group.

Film: The animated movie *An American Tail* illustrates the random and violent action of the Cossacks, although, of course, the film uses cats and mice to depict the Jews and their persecutors. Nonetheless, the film may prove a good resource for discussing and writing about the persecution of the Jews late in the nineteenth century and early in the twentieth. *Schindler's List* is perhaps the finest film on the subject of the Holocaust, but it should only be viewed by mature students and adults. This film is R-rated. Be sure to get school district approval and written parent permission before showing it to students.

Boxer Rebellion

Throughout the late 1800s, a movement in China was spreading to destroy Western and Japanese influence in the country. Out of this movement sprang the Boxer Rebellion.

A secret organization called *Yihequan* (Righteous and Harmonious Fists), a group that stemmed from the White Lotus sect, began the movement in opposition to the Manchus, the rulers of China. The organization's members were nicknamed Boxers by the Westerners because of their practice of gymnastics and other calisthenics. By the 1890s, the Boxers had begun to oppose all foreign influence in their homeland. Many Chinese supported these anti-foreign sentiments, and even the Manchus did in secret.

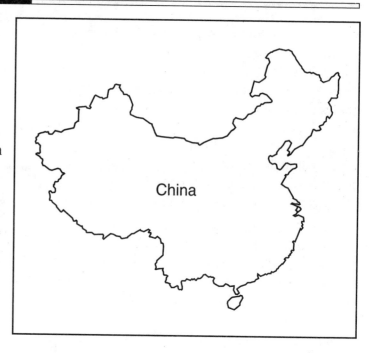

In 1900, the Boxers banded together to wipe out foreign influence in any way they could. They murdered foreigners, missionaries, Chinese Christians, and supporters of foreign ideas, and they burned countless homes, schools, and churches. Foreign diplomats became alarmed at their actions and called for troops to combat the Boxers. At this, the Manchus declared war against all foreign powers. From June 21 to August 14, 1900, Boxers and military troops attacked the residences of foreign diplomats in Beijing. The diplomats, Chinese Christians, and foreign civilians resisted their attacks until a force from eight foreign nations arrived and squelched the uprising.

In the following year, the Manchus and eleven other nations signed a pact called The Boxer Protocol. China agreed to punish and execute several leaders of the uprising as well as to pay approximately $330 million in damages. Some of this money was returned by the United States in 1908 under the condition it would be used for education in China. In later years, Japan and Britain followed America's lead and did the same.

Suggested Activities

Geography: Locate China, Japan, Britain, and the United States on a map.

Research: Read about the Manchus and their government. Determine what facets of their government troubled the Boxers. Also research to learn about Western influence in China today. A great deal has changed over the course of the twentieth century, and Western influence can be seen in many ways around the world.

Discuss: The Boxers were greatly opposed to Western influence. Ask the students to discuss why this was so and to share their own feelings and ideas about foreign influence on a nation. Ask them to put themselves in place of the Boxers and others around the world who are angered by foreign influence.

Empress in China

The year 1908 saw the death of one of the most manipulative and cruelest leaders of all time. It is believed by many that she was murdered for her treachery. Her name was Empress Dowager T'zu-hsi (Cixi).

Born in 1835, T'zu-hsi was Emperor Hsien Feng's concubine. She bore him a son, and from this time became his favorite of all the concubines. It is said that as early as 1851, she had effective control of the imperial court. At the Emperor's death in 1862, she stole his royal seal. The seal was required for all documents so that they could be officially signed. Without the seal, members of the court could not take over the monarchy. With the aid of the seal, T'zu-hsi was able to steal the Emperor's royal seat and become Empress herself.

Empress T'zu-hsi

While her son was young, the Empress ruled alone. In 1875, her child died of the smallpox. The Empress appointed her nephew, Kuang Hsu, as the heir, but she continued to rule. When Kuang Hsu was 21 and able to rule on his own, she used her influence in court to have him taken prisoner when he tried to make reforms.

At the turn of the century, the Empress was in full support of the Boxer Rebellion (page 76) because she wanted to return China to the days before there was any European influence. Personal control was always her goal. She managed to defeat all attempts at modernization and change throughout her very long rule.

During her time, the Empress was known for her love of the theater. She greatly enjoyed acting in plays, and it was said that she always looked as though she were ready for the stage. Photographs of her show her heavily made up.

When she was an old woman, it became clear that she was going to die. She wished to control China until the very end, and therefore she had Kuang Hsu executed so that he would die before her. She then appointed Pu Yi, who was two years old, as her successor. Pu Yi was the final emperor of China.

Suggested Activities

History: Read about the rule of Pu Yi and how the succession of emperors in China came to an end.

Women: Although cruel, Empress T'zu-hsi is notable as a woman who ruled in a world largely run by men. Learn about other female world leaders and the variety of ways in which they have governed.

Writing: The Empress's treachery, although heinous, makes for an interesting story. Have the students write short stories or plays that tell of the life of T'zu-hsi.

The Commonwealth of Australia

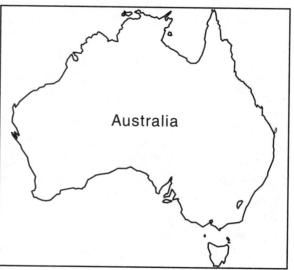

Australia is the only country that is also a continent. Aborigines have been living in Australia for at least 40,000 years, but whites, who comprise most of the population today, first arrived there in 1788 as prisoners exiled to the new colonies owned by Great Britain. Most of these prisoners were debtors and petty criminals.

In the mid-nineteenth century, Australia was explored, and in 1851, gold was discovered. In 10 years, the population of 400,000 grew to 1,100,000; the bulk of the rise was due to goldseekers who did not find enough gold to earn their passages home. Meanwhile, convicts were still shipped to the colonies until 1868. More than 160,000 convicts were sent in all.

As the population grew, inevitably so did the call for self-government. Britain granted self-government to most of the colonies in Australia but maintained the management of defense and foreign relations. All the colonies were self-governed by 1890.

In the next decade, there was growing support for a union of the colonies. The people felt that they would be better off as a single nation with a unified government so that they could deal with their common problems and help one another. A constitution was drawn up in 1897 and 1898, and in 1898 and 1899 the people approved it. Britain gave its approval in 1900. The colonies became the six states of a new nation on January 1, 1901. The Commonwealth of Australia was born.

Today, Australia is a farming and mining nation with a strong support for the arts. There is a high standard of living for most Australians. Although Australia is the sixth-largest country in terms of landmass, it is sparsely populated with an average of six people per square mile (two per square kilometer) and a population of about 20 million. Its climate is dry and sunny and the landscape features many large, open spaces. Much of the population lives along the southeastern coast. Sydney and Melbourne, its two largest cities, can be found there. Canberra, its capital, is slightly inland.

The official language of Australia is English, and its government is a constitutional monarchy. The monarch of England is the head of state.

One of the most famous landmarks of Australia is the Sydney Opera House. One of its most famous personalities is Olivia Newton John, a popular singer of the 1970s and 1980s.

Australia's flag is comprised of the British Union flag, one large star representing the nation's states and territories and five stars depicting the Southern Cross constellation.

Suggested Activities

Cartography: Have the students make maps of Australia, showing its states and territories as well as its major geological features.

Favorite Australians: Research to find the names and histories of some of Australia's most famous citizens.

Debate: Hold a debate on the topic of international relocation for prisoners. Is it justified and humane?

Long Live the Queen

It was a long life indeed for Queen Victoria, who ruled from 1837 until her death on January 22, 1901. Born in 1819, her reign began at the death of William IV. Three years after she was crowned, she married Albert, prince of Saxe-Coburg-Gotha. He lived until 1861. Victoria's name is used to describe the period of time during which she reigned, its characteristics, and its attitudes. Much of it died along with her at the dawning of the twentieth century.

Queen Victoria

At birth, Victoria's arrival was not particularly noteworthy—it was merely a series of deaths and changes that brought her to reign. However, her reign became one of the longest and most influential in Britain's history. Crowned Queen of England and Ireland and Empress of India, Victoria dominated the middle and latter nineteenth century. Her reign can be seen roughly in two parts, each approximately 30 years. The first was characterized by a rapid growth in industry; a swelling of the population; the rising of a strong, industrial middle class; and only moderate political reforms. There was prosperity and stability. The nation was complacent, happy in its good fortune. The masses strongly supported national virtues which became linked indelibly with the Victorian Age: industriousness, piety, charity, and moral righteousness. Victorians saw themselves as dramatically improved over their ancestors in intelligence and morality.

The second half of Victoria's reign is characterized by a decline in the birth rate, the threat of mass unemployment, economic crisis, and developments in science that threatened longstanding religious beliefs. Poverty, the plight of the working class, child labor, conflict among the classes—these became the themes of the later years. The literature of Charles Dickens deals extensively with these themes.

Part of the shift in focus during the Victorian Age was due to the publication of Darwin's *Origin of Species*. Religious views were shaken and conflicts arose. Darwin, as well as others, was hurrying the destruction of traditional Victorian values. In addition, the rise in the middle class created even greater tensions and disparity within the working class.

At the death of Victoria in 1901, traditional values were already at a very low ebb. The woman and the age came to a close. A new era was dawning, and rigid morality would have no part in it.

Victoria was succeeded by her son Edward VII, who ruled throughout the rest of the decade.

Suggested Activities

Reading: Lytton Strachey's *Queen Victoria* (Harcourt Brace Jovanovich) was a groundbreaking biography when it was published in 1921. Read excerpts of it to the class. Also read any number of works that come from the Victorian Age. Dickens' novels are considered by many to be the classic works of Victorian England.

Discussion: Lead the class in a discussion of the Victorian Age versus the Golden Age of the twentieth century.

Evans and Knossos

British archeologist and numismatist (student of coins and medals) Sir Arthur John Evans was born in Hertfordshire, England, in July of 1851. He received an extensive education and later spent many years in the Balkans studying archeological sites.

In the ensuing years, Evans developed a great interest in the Mycenean culture of Ancient Greece. He was convinced that he would find the origins of the civilization on Crete, Greece's largest island. He also believed that the Myceneans had a system of writing that was previously unknown.

Evans began excavations at the site of the Palace of King Minos at Knossos, Crete, in 1908. He uncovered the 3,000-year-old palace, believed to be the Labyrinth found in the myth of Theseus. Over the next twenty-five years, he also discovered many beautiful artifacts of the Bronze Age as well as evidence of two pictographic systems of writing. The archeologist's work shed much light on the cultures of that time and place. Evans called this culture Minoan after King Minos. His work demonstrated that Minoan Crete was the center of a sea empire, connected with Tiryns and Mycenae. He also learned that the culture was in regular contact with Egypt and Europe for almost 1,000 years. In about 1400 B.C., the civilization came to an abrupt end. It is unclear what became of it, although it is known that Romans invaded the island around 66 B.C. and made Crete a province.

The Minoan culture is one of the first European civilizations. It began nearly 5,000 years ago, and Crete was, indeed, its birthplace. The first people came from Asia Minor (now Turkey), and over the course of 3,000 years, developed an advanced culture. The Minoan culture made exemplary advances in engineering, architecture, and art.

In 1911, Evans was knighted for the archeological work he had done. He died in 1941.

Suggested Activity

Archeology: The science of archeology is painstaking. The work must be done carefully and over a period of time. In order for your students to learn about archeology firsthand, develop a site on which they can dig. Within the sand or dirt, bury a variety of objects that the students can later uncover. Chart your work carefully! Provide the students with information that will lead them to the site. Allow them to dig just as an archeologist might. If possible, invite an archeologist to be a part of your excavation and to share with the students some archaeological information.

Marie Curie and the Nobel Prize

Marie Curie was born Marja Sklodowska in Warsaw, Poland, on November 7, 1867. Her father was a teacher of high school physics. In 1891, she went to the Sorbonne in Paris, changed her name to Marie, and studied physics. She passed the examinations to receive her degree in just two years, and she ranked first in her class. One year later, she met Pierre Curie, and they were married in 1895.

At the time Marie Curie was involved in her studies, there were discoveries being made in radiation that interested her. She began to study uranium radiation. She combined her husband's work in piezoelectric techniques with her own research, measuring radiation in pitchblende, a uranium-containing ore. Out of this work, Marie coined the term "radioactive." In a short time, Pierre terminated his own research in magnetism to join his wife in her explorations.

Marie Curie

In 1898, the Curies announced they had discovered two elements, radium and polonium. Marie named polonium after her native Poland. The Curies continued their work, and in 1903, they were awarded the Nobel Prize in physics for the discovery of radioactive elements. They shared the prize with Antoine Henri Becquerel. Marie was the first woman ever to receive a Nobel Prize.

As a direct result of their work and the Nobel Prize, Pierre was appointed a professor of physics at the University of Paris and then named to the French Academy. Marie, being a woman, was not recognized.

Pierre died in 1906, the result of a horse-cart accident. Marie continued the work on her own, and she also took over Pierre's classes. In 1911, she was awarded the Nobel Prize for chemistry. At the time, no one had ever received a second Nobel Prize. She went on to found the Curie Institute and to head the Paris Institute of Radium.

On July 4, 1934, Marie Curie died of pernicious anemia. The disease was caused by overexposure to radiation.

Marie and Pierre's daughter, Irene Joliot-Curie, became a Nobel Prize winner in 1935 for her synthesis of radioactive elements.

Suggested Activities

Radioactivity: Learn about radioactivity, what it is and what it does. How has its discovery helped human beings?

Women Scientists: Many women scientists have come to international recognition since the time of Marie Curie. Learn about other women who have made significant advances to physics, chemistry, and other sciences.

Nobel Prize: The Nobel Prize is considered one of the most prestigious in the world. To receive it once is a great honor. Being a two-time recipient demonstrates exceptional ability. Learn about the history and meaning of the award as well as the likelihood of receiving it twice.

Saint Pius X

The world of religion, like politics, is a varied one, filled with differing factions, systems of belief, and leaders. Among the most influential religious leaders is the pope of the Roman Catholic Church. The pope is the head of the Church and is also known as the bishop of Rome. He is appointed by a group of cardinals, and he governs Vatican City, a small area of land surrounding St. Peter's Church in Rome. Throughout history, the pope has demonstrated great power and influence in the politics and social state of the world at large.

Popes are chosen and then crowned. Once named as pope, he holds the position until his death. The introduction of a new pope is, therefore, not common.

In 1903, the world was given a new pope in Giuseppe Melchiorre Sarto, afterwards Pope Pius X. Born in Riese, Italy, in 1835, he went to college at Castelfranco and attended seminary at Padua. In 1858, he was ordained as a priest in the Catholic Church. Later, he was named cardinal-patriarch of Venice. During his time in that position, Pope Leo XIII died at the age of 93, and Pius was elected to the position.

The ceremony in which Pius became pope was an elaborate and colorful one, lasting more than five hours. More than 70,000 people came to see the ceremony. When one considers that this took place before the invention of television and radio, such a number of observers is astronomical.

Pope Pius X was a very conservative leader, both in religion and in politics. He stood in strong opposition to nineteenth-century scientific thought and modern intellectual liberalism. He freely condemned many modern propositions and placed a variety of books on an Index of Forbidden Books. He continuously urged the strengthening of the church from within, and he worked tirelessly against the prohibition of religious education in countries around the world which were veering toward socialism and away from religious structure.

Pius's work throughout his papacy (1903–1914) made vast differences in church organization. He restored Gregorian chant to the Catholic liturgy, he recodified canon law, and he established a new breviary (book of daily prayers) for the church as a whole.

Pius died in 1914, after 11 years of service in the papacy. He was succeeded by Pope Benedict XV.

Pope Pius X's works were recognized in the church as important and influential. As a result of them, and in accord with the Roman Catholic Church's requirements, Pius was canonized as a saint in 1954. His feast day is celebrated on August 21 each year.

Suggested Activities

Catholicism: Learn about the structure and history of the Roman Catholic Church.

Papacy: Find out about important papal leaders and the role that the papacy has played in history.

Sainthood: The Catholic Church has strict guidelines for the canonization of anyone to sainthood. Learn about those guidelines and what Pius and others did to meet them.

Panamanian Treaty

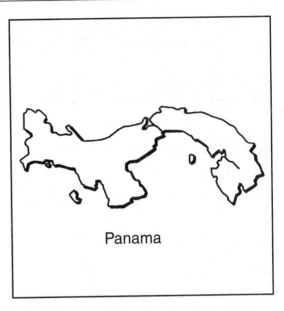

Panama

Since the time of extensive exploration in Central America in the sixteenth century, there had been international interest in finding a shortened route between the Pacific and Atlantic Oceans. The Holy Roman Emperor Charles V was the first to suggest exploration of the Isthmus of Panama as a possible canal site in 1523. A plan for creating such a canal was drawn in 1529 and another in 1534. More suggestions came as the years passed, but none was accepted or followed.

In the nineteenth century, interest flourished. The United States took surveys to determine the best route. In 1876, an international company was created to oversee the project. It received permission from the Colombian government, which was at that time in control of Panama. However, the company folded. It was followed by a French company, but it also failed. At that time, the United States began negotiations with Colombia for permission to build a canal across the Panamanian Isthmus. Colombia rejected the U.S. plan; however, Panama revolted against Colombia, and in 1903, Panama signed the Hay-Bunau-Varilla Treaty in which the U.S. guaranteed Panamanian independence and acquired a perpetual lease on a strip of land to be used for the canal. The area of land was 16 kilometers (10 miles) long. Panama received an initial payment of 10 million dollars to be followed by yearly payments of $250,000 beginning in 1913 when the canal was projected for completion. In 1936, this figure was reconfigured to $430,000, and in 1955, it was changed to two million dollars per year.

The canal opened in the summer of 1914. The cost and work were extended greatly beyond the projections; however, the canal's usefulness soon made the extra trouble seem well worth the effort.

Two new treaties signed in 1977 superceded the initial treaty of 1903. Through these treaties, Panama achieved sovereignty of the Canal Zone and control of the canal beginning in the year 2000. The United States retained the right to always defend the neutrality of the canal.

Suggested Activities

How Big Is It?: The Panama Canal, although relatively small in size, has made a tremendous difference in modern shipping. Use reference materials to find the actual dimensions of the Canal.

New Treaty: Why did Panama and the United States agree to new treaties in 1977? Research to answer this question.

Construction: Find out about the construction of the Canal and the obstacles to its completion.

Yellow Fever and Malaria: These diseases played an important role in the creation of the Canal, and they were virtually eradicated because of it. Find out why.

Nineteen Hundreds Facts and Figures

Make a copy of the chart below for each pair of students. Direct them to use the information on this page as a comparison with a chart (page 85) they will complete about the current decade.

The United States in the Nineteen Hundreds

Population: 83,822,000 (1905)

Postage: 2¢

Dozen Eggs: 27¢

Road Speed Limits: 10 mph (populated areas), 15 mph (villages), 20 mph (country roads)

Popular Books: *Peter Pan, Just So Stories, The Return of Sherlock Holmes, The Awakening, The Tale of Peter Rabbit, House of Mirth, The Souls of Black Folk, The Last of the Plainsmen, Rebecca of Sunnybrook Farm, The Call of the Wild, The Wind in the Willows, Anne of Green Gables, The Wonderful Wizard of Oz, The Turn of the Screw, Sister Carrie*

Popular Entertainers: The Barrymores (Lionel, John, and Ethel), Sarah Bernhardt, Isadora Duncan, *Ziegfeld Follies*, Maude Adams, Enrico Caruso, Victor Herbert, Harry Houdini, Arturo Toscanini, Will Rogers, Mary Pickford

Popular Songs: "In the Good Old Summertime," "Ta-Ra-Ra-Boom-De-Ay," "Sweet Adeline," "My Wild Irish Rose," "Stars and Stripes Forever," "Alexander's Ragtime Band," "Maple Leaf Rag"

Popular Movies: *The Great Train Robbery, The Life of an American Fireman, The Count of Monte Cristo, The Widow Jones, The Little Doctor, Cinderella, Skating* and other Max Linder comedies, *The Last Days of Pompeii, Carmen,* newsreels

Popular Theater: *Babes in Toyland, Peter Pan, Florodora, The Wizard of Oz, Salome, Origin of the Cake Walk*

Fashions: *(women)* Gibson Girl look, high-topped shoes, pointed toes, Louis XIV heels, leggings, spats, elaborate hats, split skirts (for riding), "pouter pigeon" blouse fronts, dropped waists, hems to the floor or just above the ankle, sashes, bows, lace, Edwardian styles; *(men)* spats, leggings, high-topped shoes, simple hats, sack suits, ties, vests, suspenders

Fads: limericks, automats, nickelodeons, the cake walk (a dance), teddy bears, comic strips

New Products: Jell-O, Dixie Cups, Maytag washing machine, Hoover vacuum, Neiman-Marcus stores, Kellogg's cornflakes, electric irons, electric toasters, Gillette safety razors, iced tea, ice-cream cones, wireless radio, sonar, metered taxicabs, garages, the Lincoln penny, airplanes, slow-motion effects in films, fountain pens

Popular Artists: Paul Cézanne, Auguste Rodin, "Ashcan" artists, Mary Cassatt, Frank Lloyd Wright (architect), Winslow Homer, Frederic Remington, James Whistler, Pablo Picasso, Henri de Toulouse-Lautrec, Paul Gauguin, Henri Matisse, Marc Chagall

Popular Writers: Anton Chekhov, G. K. Chesterton, Sir Arthur Conan Doyle, Edith Wharton, W. E. B. Du Bois, L. Frank Baum, Theodore Dreiser, Kate Douglas Wiggin, Zane Grey, Jack London, Upton Sinclair, Henry James, Mark Twain, muckrakers

Sports Stars: Dwight F. Davis, Cy Young, Ty Cobb, Honus Wagner, W. C. Grace, Marvin Hart, May Sutton, Ray C. Ewry, Jack Johnson, William Muldoon

Popular Heroes: The Wright Brothers, Louis Bleriot, Thomas Alva Edison, Albert Einstein, Captain Robert Falcon Scott, Robert Peary, Matthew Henson

Comparing the Times

With a partner, fill in the blanks on this page. Compare your answers with the information on page 84.

Year: _____

Population: _____

Postage: _____

Dozen Eggs: _____

Road Speed Limits: _____

Popular Books: _____

Popular Entertainers: _____

Popular Songs: _____

Popular Movies: _____

Popular Theater: _____

Fashions: *(women)* _____

        (men) _____

Fads: _____

New Products: _____

Popular Artists: _____

Popular Writers: _____

Sports Stars: _____

Popular Heroes: _____

Famous Firsts

In the 1900s, the United States saw the first

   . . . American Bowling Club tournament held in Chicago.

   . . . coast-to-coast crossing of America by car (65 days).

   . . . baseball World Series and home run in a World Series.

   . . . subway in New York.

   . . . American Olympics (at St. Louis).

   . . . Davis Cup in tennis.

   . . . woman arrested for smoking a cigarette in public.

   . . . neon light signs.

   . . . Rotary Club organization.

   . . . Mother's Day.

   . . . daily comic strip.

   . . . black world heavyweight boxing champion, Jack Johnson.

   . . . baseball season where spitballs were illegal.

   . . . manned flight in a heavier-than-air plane.

   . . . Ford Model T and a vehicle from the newly created General Motors.

   . . . American to play cricket for the Gentlemen of England.

   . . . permanent waves.

   . . . air-conditioned factory.

   . . . auto advertisement in a magazine.

   . . . postage stamps issued in book form.

   . . . car to be driven faster than one mile (1.6 km) per minute.

   . . . person to go over Niagara Falls in a barrel.

   . . . Tournament of Roses football game in Pasadena, California.

   . . . black woman, M. L. Walker, to serve as a bank president.

   . . . radio distress signal.

   . . . ice-cream cones.

   . . . forest fire lookout tower and watchman service.

   . . . Jewish member of the president's cabinet, Oscar S. Straus.

   . . . black to win a Rhodes scholarship, A. L. R. Locke.

   . . . Bibles placed in hotel rooms.

   . . . coin with a likeness of a president.

   . . . movie made in Los Angeles.

   . . . electric washing machine marketed.

   . . . steam-operated pressing machine.

   . . . international women's suffrage association.

          86

What Year Was That?

Check how well you remember the first decade of the twentieth century by circling the correct year for each event.

1. The Olympic games are held in Paris during the World Exhibition.
   1900   1901   1902

2. Revolution breaks out in Russia.
   1903   1904   1905

3. France is granted a mandate over Morocco.
   1905   1906   1907

4. Roosevelt wins the Nobel Prize for helping to end the Russo-Japanese War.
   1906   1907   1908

5. The first Model T is produced.
   1906   1907   1908

6. The first Tour de France race is held.
   1902   1903   1904

7. The Goodwill Cruise is sent by President Roosevelt to sail around the world.
   1905   1906   1907

8. Peary and Henson reach the North Pole.
   1907   1908   1909

9. A devastating earthquake strikes San Francisco.
   1905   1906   1907

10. The Boxer Rebellion erupts.
    1900   1901   1902

11. Louis Blériot flies across the English Channel.
    1907   1908   1909

12. The Pennsylvania Coal Strike leads to a coal shortage across the United States.
    1900   1901   1902

13. Captain Scott explores the Antarctic.
    1903   1904   1905

14. The Wright Brothers fly near Kittyhawk.
    1901   1902   1903

15. Queen Victoria of England dies.
    1900   1901   1902

16. The Boer War ends.
    1900   1901   1902

17. The first World Series is held.
    1901   1902   1903

18. President McKinley is assassinated.
    1900   1901   1902

19. *The Tale of Peter Rabbit* is published.
    1902   1903   1904

20. William Howard Taft is elected president.
    1907   1908   1909

Into the 'Teens

The first decade of the twentieth century was a time of hope and progressive thinking mixed with political turmoil and the growing threat of war. The next decade would see that threat become a reality.

World War I began as a local war between Austria-Hungary and Serbia. As a result of conflicts in the Balkan states, the rise of nationalism, and a series of international alliances, it rapidly became a general European struggle. Eventually, it became a global war involving 32 nations. The 28 nations known as the Allies and Associated Powers included Great Britain, France, Russia, and, eventually, the United States. The Central Powers consisted of Germany, Austria-Hungary, Turkey, and Bulgaria. Acts of heroism and tragedy filled the newspapers daily, and people on the homefronts focused their energies on "helping the cause" in whatever ways they could.

Heroes and villains came to the forefront throughout the war and its aftermath. Frequently mentioned names include Lenin, Rasputin, Lloyd George, Kitchener, Von Hindenburg, Mata Hari, the Kaiser, Czar Nicholas II, Trotsky, Stalin, the Red Baron, Pershing, Baruch, Hoover, and Wilson.

The World War also brought an influx of advanced technology, including tanks, submarines, poison gas, long-range bombers, and fighter planes. Much of the war, however, was fought in the trenches, which were also used for the first time during these battles.

Power in Europe and Russia shifted dramatically both during the Great War and as a result of it. New leaders offered hope to the impoverished and battle-scarred masses. However, lingering resentments and unresolved turmoil perpetuated the conflict, and future decades would see the results.

Of course, war was not the only thing of significance to happen during the 'teens. Labor disputes and the push for women's rights built to critical masses, bringing about dramatic changes in the workplace and the home. By the end of the decade, victory came to the suffragists, and labor unions and labor laws brought new and better conditions to the labor force.

Electronic and other inventions continued to increase during the first decade and into the 'teens. Inventor Thomas Alva Edison developed talking pictures which would soon revolutionize the entertainment industry. In Hollywood, California, a film mecca was begun by Cecil B. De Mille. A small group of actors began a new company, United Artists, in order to produce their own films. The world of entertainment grew rapidly, and people began to flock to the theaters.

With the end of the war and the decade, the world began to rebuild itself and to hope for a better future. Things looked brighter as the 'teens drew to a close. People were ready to let the Roaring Twenties begin.

Literature Connections

One surefire way to interest students in a specific topic is through the use of literature. Read through the annotated bibliography to decide which pieces of literature you might like to use with your class. Helpful suggestions for extending the books follow each description.

The Call of the Wild by Jack London (1903)

The family dog, Buck, is stolen from his comfortable home and sold into service as a Klondike sled dog. Suffering abuses at human hands and by his fellow dogs, his basic nature begins to unleash itself, and he is able to fight with killer instincts. He eventually becomes leader of the sled-dog team. Later, he finds himself with a kind and loving master, John Thorton, whom he grows to love. When Thorton is killed, Buck's primal instincts completely take him over, and he becomes the leader of a wolf pack, living free in the wild.

Extensions:

Discussion Questions—Assess students' comprehension and understanding with some discussion questions. For example, why is Buck abducted? What is "the call of the wild"? Why does Buck love John Thorton? Why does he return each year to the scene of Thorton's death?

Mapping—Draw maps that show Buck's travels from California to the wild at the novel's end.

Dog Sleds—Find out about dogsleds and how they are operated. Read about the Iditarod dogsled race that takes place in Alaska each March.

Comparisons—Compare the nature and physicality of domesticated dogs and wolves. Create a chart that shows the similarities and differences between the two.

Two Breeds—Buck is half St. Bernard and half Scottish sheepdog. Learn about the two breeds and what qualities they might have that aid Buck in his adventures.

The Hounds of the Baskervilles by Sir Arthur Conan Doyle (1902)

One of many classic Sherlock Holmes mysteries, *The Hounds of the Baskervilles* finds the hero dealing with the seemingly supernatural to solve his case. Any of Conan Doyle's stories can be studied for both their exciting mysteries and also for their excellent depictions of England at the turn of the century. In all, Conan Doyle wrote four Holmes novels and 56 short stories.

Extensions:

Mysteries—Instruct student groups to write original mystery stories for the Holmes character.

Ratiocination—This is a term coined by Edgar Allan Poe, credited with writing the first detective novel in which logical problem-solving and deduction (ratiocination) are used to solve the mystery. Discuss ratiocination and provide several examples from the book as well as from other classic detective stories. Instruct students to each create a ratiocination example of their own.

London—Study London at the turn of the century and compare it to Conan Doyle's depiction.

Becoming Holmes—Let student teams create mysteries for another team to solve. These can be written or acted. Instruct them to apply the same techniques used by Sherlock Holmes.

One More to Read

The Wind in the Willows by Kenneth Grahame (1908)

This book of Mr. Toad and his cronies is pure fantasy, but it can be read with an eye for the time since the animal characters have human characteristics and dwell in human-like settings.

Literature Connections *(cont.)*

Peter Pan, or The Boy Who Wouldn't Grow Up by James M. Barrie (1904)

Peter Pan, the hero, has long ago escaped to Never-Never-Land where he leads a group of lost children. Peter meets the Darling children while searching for his missing shadow, and they decide to join him in Never-Never-Land. The children have many adventures there, particularly with Captain Hook, Peter's archenemy. They are protected, however, by a pixie named Tinker Bell, and an Indian princess, Tiger Lily. When the children are eventually saved from Captain Hook, they decide they must return home. Peter chooses not to go with them, desiring to remain in Never-Never-Land where he can avoid growing up. Wendy agrees to return for a visit each year.

This classic tale, although fantasy, will provide a sense of time and place for the turn of the century.

Extensions:

Growing Up—Discuss what it means to grow up. Have the students write papers explaining their thoughts on the subject. Create a comparison chart with "Child" and "Grown up" as the headers.

Pan—Learn about the mythological character of Pan. How is Peter like or unlike him?

Pirates—There was a time when the existence of pirates created a general fear across the seas. Students may be surprised to learn that there are pirates even today. Research the history of pirates, especially what they were like and did around the turn of the century.

Childhood—Social conceptions of childhood have changed significantly over the years. Learn about how people generally viewed children at the time of the novel, as well as what adults expected from them. Also learn how children dressed (page 67), what they did for amusement, what school was like for them, and how they may have been disciplined.

Stories—Let students write stories, using the information from the previous activity. In their stories, they can place themselves circa 1900 and tell about their experiences as a child.

Anne of Green Gables by Lucy Maud Montgomery (1908)

This and the subsequent novels in the series depict the early years of the twentieth century with great skill and clarity. They are "must reads," not only for the time but for the endearing character of Anne Shirley, the orphan girl who finds her home and haven at Green Gables farm. Anne's world is rich with imagination, and her exuberance and joy affect everyone around her.

Extensions

PE Island—The Anne novels take place on Prince Edward Island, Canada, circa 1900. Study P.E.I. (as Anne calls it) and compare its true history and locales with those of the novel.

Imagination—Part of what makes Anne so delightful is her full imagination. Spend some classtime daydreaming about an imaginary world, and let the students write what they imagine.

Bosom Friends—Anne's "bosom friend" is Diana Wright. Have the students tell about their own bosom friends in character studies they write.

One More to Read

On the Banks of the Bayou by Roger Lea MacBride (1998)

This and the others in the series tell the story of Rose Wilder Lane, daughter of Laura Ingalls Wilder. They take place just before and after the turn of the century. This book, in particular, gives a full sense of the socio-political climate in the first decade.

Writing Prompts

Use these suggestions for journal writing or for extended writing assignments. Some research or discussion may be appropriate before adding a particular topic.

- Write a firsthand narrative as though you are a witness to the shooting of President McKinley.

- You are a member of the suffragette movement. Write a speech in support of the cause.

- You are at a rally with Eugene Debs as the keynote speaker. What do you think of him? How do you feel and react?

- Coal miners in Pennsylvania are striking, and your family is nearly without coal. A storm is about to occur. How do you feel about the strikers? What do you think of labor unions?

- Queen Liliuokalani of Hawaii saw the end of Hawaii's monarchy. She is also remembered as a writer of songs. Write the lyrics to a song in tribute to her and her beautiful land.

- The teddy bear is named for President Theodore Roosevelt. Invent a toy named after the current president. Describe your toy and create a slogan to sell it.

- Imagine being your age at the turn of the century, January 1, 1900. Write a diary entry for that day.

- You are a Russian peasant demonstrating outside the czar's palace with Father Gapon. Tell about what happens that day.

- Imagine you are leaving your native land on a boat heading for America. Write a journal entry (or entries), telling what you feel and think as you cross the Atlantic.

- You are playing with your friends in the streets of your Kansas town when you see a tall woman dressed in black and carrying a hatchet march angrily into a local saloon. You hear crashes, bangs, and the sound of glass breaking. You walk to the door to peek inside, and you see that the woman is Carry Nation. Write what you observe.

- You are listening to a debate between Booker T. Washington and W. E. B. Du Bois on education. What do they have to say? What do you think?

- You and your family have survived the earthquake and fires in San Francisco in 1906. Tell about your experiences.

- You are a student at Radcliffe College, taking classes with a young blind and deaf woman named Helen Keller. How do you imagine she is able to study and to learn?

- Beatrix Potter gave animals human characteristics. Write an original tale of an animal that has some human qualities.

- The Tour de France is riding through your town! Describe the experience.

- Attending an art museum, you see the work of Pablo Picasso for the first time. Describe it and what you think.

- You are in a Grafton church in 1908, celebrating the first Mother's Day. Describe the service.

Me in 1900

Imagine yourself at your current age in 1900. Complete the following prompts, using what you imagine to fill in the blanks.

Where I live: _____

_____

_____

What my home is like: _____

_____

_____

_____

What I do when I get up in the morning: _____

_____

_____

What a typical school day is like: _____

_____

_____

What I do for fun: _____

_____

_____

My chores: _____

_____

_____

How my family and I spend our evenings: _____

_____

Buzzwords

New inventions, habits, lifestyles, and occupations cause people to invent new words. The first decade of the new century was no exception. Listed below are some of the words and phrases that came into popular use throughout the decade.

airspeed: This is the speed of an aircraft determined by its relationship with the air instead of the ground.

bonehead: This expression means a stupid or ignorant person, someone who has only bone and no brains in his or her head.

borderline: This word for boundary or dividing line can also mean a person or thing on the edge.

Boy Scout: This name is used for a young individual belonging to a group begun by Robert Baden-Powell, the purpose of which was to teach self-reliance, good citizenship, and outdoor skills.

buffer zone: This refers to an independent and neutral place, person, or circumstance located between two antagonistic places, people, or circumstances.

garage: This is a shelter or storage facility for an automobile.

grandfather clause: The constitutions of some southern states contained a provision intended to prevent blacks from voting. It read, "No person shall vote in this state if he is unable to read and write, unless his father or grandfather was a voter before 1867."

recessive: This word means anything that tends to go backward or recede.

right wing: This usually refers to those holding extremely conservative political views.

rip cord: This is a rope fastened to the gas bag of a balloon or dirigible so that pulling it will open the bag, release the gas, and cause descent. It is also a rope used for opening a parachute during descent.

Rocky Mountain spotted fever: This acute, infectious disease is caused by *Rickettsia* (a microorganism) from ticks found in the area around the Rocky Mountains. It causes pain, fever, and spotty, red skin blemishes.

scrimmage line: This is an imaginary line in football on which the ball sits at the beginning of each play and along which players on both teams line up.

septic tank: This refers to a tank in which waste matter decomposes through the action of bacteria.

turtleneck: This is a high collar that folds over and fits snugly around the neck.

wireless: This is a telegraph system that sends sound signals by radio waves.

world power: This refers to any nation or organization with enough power to have influence around the world.

world war: This term means war among several countries of the world.

worthwhile: This refers to anything valuable or important enough to repay the time, effort, or money spent in obtaining it.

Software in the Classroom

More and more software is finding its way into the classroom. Many of the multimedia packages allow students to access photos, speeches, film clips, maps, and newspapers of various eras in history. Although a program may not be written specifically for the topic you are studying, existing software may be adapted for your purposes. To get maximum use from these programs and to learn how to keep up with technology, try some of the suggestions below.

Software

American Heritage: The History of the United States for Young People. Byron Preiss Multimedia

American History CD. Multi-Educator

Compton's Encyclopedia of American History. McGraw Hill

Compton's Interactive Encyclopedia. Compton's New Media, Inc.

The Cruncher. Microsoft Works

Encarta (various editions). Microsoft Home

Ideas That Changed the World. Ice Publishing

Our Times: Multimedia Encyclopedia of the 20th Century (Vicarious Points of View Series 2.0). Scholastic

Presidents: A Picture History of Our Nation. National Geographic

Time Almanac. Compact Publishing (available through Broderbund, 800-922-9204)

Time Traveler CD! Orange Cherry

TimeLiner. Tom Snyder Productions (800-342-0236)

Vital Links. Educational Resources (includes videodisc and audio cassette)

Where in America's Past Is Carmen Sandiego? Broderbund

Using the Programs

After the initial excitement of using a new computer program wears off, you can still motivate students by letting them use the programs in different ways.

1. Print out a copy of a time line for the first decade for each group of students. Assign each group a different topic—for example, entertainment or politics. Direct the groups to research their topics and add text and pictures to their time lines.

2. Let each pair of students choose a specific photo from the first decade of the twentieth century. Have them research the person or event and write a news story to go with it.

3. If you do not have enough computers in your classroom, hook your computer to a television screen for whole-class activities and let the students take turns typing. Keep a kitchen timer handy. For more ideas, see *Managing Technology in the Classroom* (Teacher Created Materials #517), *Managing Technology in the One Computer Classroom* (Teacher Created Materials #2457), or the booklet *101+ Ways to Use a Computer in the Classroom* (Oxbow Creek Technology Committee, Oxbow Creek School, 6050 109th Avenue N, Champlin, MN 55316).

Internet

If you have access to the Internet, let the students search for related information. First ask the students to brainstorm a list of keywords or topics. Use a Web browser like *Alta Vista* or *Web Crawler* to search for sites. Facts, pictures, and sound clips are only a click away. As an alternative, you may wish to preview sites and provide students with a list of URLs for access. (**Note:** If the students do the searching, you may wish to install a filtering program, like *SurfWatch* from Spyglass, to limit access to objectionable material. Check with your Internet service provider.)

Bibliography

Aaseng, Nathan. *You Are the President.* Oliver Press, Inc., 1994.

Adler, Susan S. *Meet Samantha: An American Girl.* Pleasant Company, 1986.

Davis, Kenneth C. *Don't Know Much About History.* Crown Publishers, 1990.

Denam, Cherry. *The History Puzzle: An Interactive Visual Time Line.* Turner Publishing, 1995.

Doyle, Sir Arthur Conan. *The Complete Sherlock Holmes.* Doubleday, 1930.

Duden, Jane. *Timelines.* Crestwood House, 1989.

English, June. *Transportation: Automobiles to Zeppelins.* Scholastic, 1995.

Felder, Deborah G. *The Kids' World Almanac of History.* Pharos Books, 1991.

Grahame, Kenneth. *The Wind in the Willows.* Watermill, 1980.

Grun, Bernard. *The Timetables of History.* Simon and Schuster, 1991.

Hakim, Joy. *All the People.* Oxford University Press, 1995.

Hartley, L. P. *The Go-Between.* Stein and Day, 1984.

Hopkinson, Christina. *The Usborne History of the Twentieth Century.* Usborne Publishing, 1993.

Kranz, Rachel. *The Biographical Dictionary of Black Americans.* Facts on File, 1992.

Lane, Rose Wilder. *Old Home Town.* University of Nebraska Press, 1985.

London, Jack. *The Call of the Wild.* Watermill, 1980.

MacBride, Roger Lea. *On the Banks of the Bayou.* HarperCollins, 1998.

Montgomery, L. M. *Anne of Green Gables.* Scholastic, 1989.

————*The Oxford Children's Book of Famous People.* Oxford University Press, 1994.

Potter, Beatrix. *The Complete Tales of Beatrix Potter.* Penguin Group, 1989.

Rubel, David. *The Scholastic Encyclopedia of the Presidents and Their Times.* Scholastic, 1994.

————*The United States in the 20th Century.* Scholastic, 1995.

Sharman, Margaret. *Take Ten Years: 1900s, the First Decade.* Steck-Vaughn, 1994.

Skarmeas, Nancy. *First Ladies of the White House.* Ideals Publications, 1995.

Smith, Carter. *Presidents in a Time of Change.* The Millbrook Press, 1993.

Tames, Richard. *Picture History of the 20th Century: 1900–1919.* Franklin Watts, 1991.

————*What Happened Next?: Great Events.* Franklin Watts, 1995.

Whiteley, Opal. *Opal: Journey of an Understanding Heart.* Crown, 1984.

Teacher Created Materials

#064 *Share the Olympic Dream*

#069 *Elections*

#234 *Thematic Unit: Immigration*

#517 *Managing Technology in the Classroom*

#605 *Interdisciplinary Unit: Heroes*

#2313 *Social Studies Games*

#2601 *20th Century Quiz Book*

Answer Key

page 21

Speak softly and carry a big stick.: This was the basis of Roosevelt's policy in diplomatic affairs. He did not wish to outwardly threaten other countries; however, the "big stick" refers to the implied threat of war he could use as leverage in acquiring treaties with other nations.

muckraker: In an April 1906 speech, Roosevelt denounced writers he believed wrote about sensational topics purely for the sake of sensationalism. He said the writers " . . . could look no way but downward with the muckrake in his hand . . . [and continue] to rake himself the filth off the floor." Writers who saw themselves as reformers took the word "muckraker" as their badge of honor.

square deal: In a speech given on September 9, 1903, Roosevelt said, "We must treat each man on his own worth and merit as a man." The square deal referred to the fair way in which each man should be treated, given no more or no less than his own merit warranted. He did not believe in favors for the rich or handouts for the poor.

one of the governing class: Early in life, Roosevelt wanted to go into the world of politics. People in his social position generally refrained from doing so. However, he said that he wanted to become a member "of the governing class," allowing him a voice in growth and governmental change.

Rough Riders: The Rough Riders were a group of cowboy and socialite friends Roosevelt organized under the U.S. Volunteer Cavalry. In 1898, the Rough Riders joined other troops in Cuba. Their battle at San Juan Hill made them legendary.

Bully!: This was Roosevelt's favorite exclamation of joy and approval. It became synonymous with his name. He did not coin the expression, but he made it popular.

Fear God and take your own part.: During Woodrow Wilson's presidency, Roosevelt became exasperated with Wilson's desire for peace at all costs. In the face of international turmoil and eventual world war, Roosevelt made this famous statement as an expression that we should always be prepared, especially for war.

grape juice diplomacy: Again, frustrated with Wilson's government, Roosevelt used this expression to refer to Wilson's Secretary of State, William Jennings Bryan, a pacifist who drank no alcohol. This was considered ridiculous by Roosevelt, hence the expression.

page 27

1. 36
2. 12,713,325
3. 1,853
4. 463
5. 476 (election of 1904)
6. 19,278,080
7. 60%
8. 71%

page 37

1. i
2. e
3. a
4. j
5. h
6. b
7. g
8. c
9. d
10. f

page 44

a. catcher
b. batter
c. pitcher
d. first baseman
e. second baseman
f. third baseman
g. shortstop
h. right fielder
i. center fielder
j. left fielder
k. umpire

page 52

passenger—up and down. Even though the train is travelling at 50 m.p.h., those inside the train don't feel the effects of that movement. They view their fellow passengers in the same way one would view others on stable ground. Therefore, the ball appears to be acting "normally," or as one would assume it would.

person on the platform—in a parabola (upside-down horseshoe). As the child (in the train) approaches the station, he/she throws the balls upward. To the person standing on the platform (and, therefore, not moving), the ball appears to not only be going upward, but also to be going forward (since it, being inside the train, is moving 50 m.p.h., from the person on the platform's perspective). The ball appears to continue along this upward arc until it begins to fall; at that point, it is on a downward arc. Thus, a parabola.

passenger on a train passing in the opposite direction—a very wide parabola. Same idea as above, only more exaggerated. The passenger sees the ball going upward in the approaching train. Because of the combined speed of the two trains, the ball (from the approaching train's passenger's perspective) appears to be traveling forward as it ascends; then as the trains pass and the ball falls, the ball appears to be whizzing past (at 100 m.p.h.) as it descends.

page 87

1. 1900	11. 1909
2. 1905	12. 1902
3. 1906	13. 1904
4. 1906	14. 1903
5. 1908	15. 1901
6. 1903	16. 1902
7. 1907	17. 1903
8. 1909	18. 1901
9. 1906	19. 1902
10. 1900	20. 1908

96